The
Sewing Machine
as a
Creative Tool

Karen Bakke is Assistant Professor of Environmental Arts at the College for Human Development, Syracuse University. She has exhibited her weavings, sewn drawings, and quilted pieces in numerous museums and art galleries and her work has been featured in *Ladies Home Journal Needle and Craft Magazine.* She is well known for her commissioned work in hangings and liturgical banners.

THE CREATIVE HANDCRAFTS SERIES

The Sewing Machine as a Creative Tool

KAREN BAKKE

A SPECTRUM BOOK

PRENTICE-HALL, INC., ENGLEWOOD CLIFFS, NEW JERSEY

Library of Congress Cataloging in Publication Data

Bakke, Karen.
    The sewing machine as a creative tool.

    (The Creative handcrafts series)   (A Spectrum Book)
    Bibliography: p.
    Includes index.
    1. Sewing. 2. Needlework. I. Title.
TT713.B34   746.4'028   75-26868
ISBN 0-13-807255-8
ISBN 0-13-807248-5 pbk.

Frontispiece: *Portrait of the artist
in her super-flash hat.* Sewing machine
drawing, appliqué, and collage (author).

© 1976 by Prentice-Hall, Inc.
Englewood Cliffs, New Jersey

A SPECTRUM BOOK

10 9 8 7 6 5 4 3 2 1

Printed in the United States of America

Prentice-Hall International, Inc. (*London*)
Prentice-Hall of Australia Pty., Ltd. (*Sydney*)
Prentice-Hall of Canada, Ltd. (*Toronto*)
Prentice-Hall of India Private Limited (*New Delhi*)
Prentice-Hall of Japan, Inc. (*Tokyo*)
Prentice-Hall of Southeast Asia (Pte.) Ltd. (*Singapore*)

To Larry and Larry

Contents

ix

Preface

"But how did you come to do this kind of work, my dear?"

Like the automobile or abstract expressionism, it was "in the air," and I was one of many to pick it out—partly because of my dislike of the sewing machine and what one did with it. I was the scourge of the home economics departments in junior high and high school. I had great patience in achieving an artistic look for aprons and skirts and in re-embroidering the fabric of the purple-striped baby-doll pajamas and the kelly green apron, but the nitty-gritty of the pieces—getting the sleeves in correctly and not sewing part of the front to the side seam because I had neglected to straighten a rather large fold—eluded me. After cutting out and embellishing, I was done with the piece. So my career in structured sewing was, by very mutual consent, limited. However, I had retained a fondness for the sewing machine, derived from hours and hours of making clothes for Katie and Faye Ann, my favorite dolls. Their clothes

xi

were works of art, with lots of sewn lines, patches, laces, and riots of colors and buttons. Although I couldn't put in a deadly serious waistband, for heaven's sake, I could, nonetheless, construct elaborately decorated head pieces for poor Faye Ann to cover her broken head. So a little germ remained of the fun one could have with a sewing machine.

When I got married in 1964, our first purchase was a sewing machine—a big thing on one graduate assistantship income. I had ideas of becoming a great earth-mother type—baking all our bread and making all our clothes. My baking consisted of one apple pie—without peeling the apples (to save time)—and my sewing consisted of thousands of appliqué pieces, drawings, and generally delightful sewn bits, with no rhyme or reason. My career in nonsewing had begun in earnest, and it continues to this day.

Acknowledgments

The task of putting this book together was made considerably easier by the help and encouragement of family and friends. Thanks to my many students at Syracuse University, who supplied many of the worked examples. Thanks also to my delightful sister Pat Nelson, who helped clarify ideas, and to my parents, Loren and Ann Mork, who always hoped I would learn to sew and so provided much encouragement. And, finally, the most special thanks and armloads of gratitude to my husband, Dr. Larry Bakke, who not only helped with the conception of the project but also did most of the photography and lived with the mess in the living room for the duration of the writing.

Introduction

Elias Howe, Jr., and Isaac Singer, whose names are relatively unfamiliar to the general populace, may have helped to revolutionize the world economic situation in terms of the commercial manufacture of many kinds of textile goods. For it was thcy who, in the early 1850s, put the finishing touches on the invention of the sewing machine with the eye in the end of the needle.

Today's standard home sewing machine, based on their earlier models, is one of the most versatile tools in existence. However, it is a tool whose use has long been rigidly compartmentalized. It has been so closely associated with the production of articles such as standard garments and curtains that seldom have all its wonderful capabilities been investigated. It is really a marvelously versatile machine; and this book will explore some of the machine's possibilities, such as appliqué, patchwork, drawing, and quilting, areas that are seldom mentioned in relation to the sewing machine.

There is little tradition in the creative use of the sewing machine. (There are a number of very sophisticated embroidery machines that are used in industry, but the home sewer or craftsperson almost never has access to these.) An open attitude toward this type of sewing machine work should prevail—an attitude that "anything goes" and that there is no right or wrong way to approach this work. Serendipity is often the creative sewer's best friend! There are many technical aids listed in this book, but these are not to be taken necessarily as absolutes. It is hoped that this book will merely open the door to more ideas and ways of approaching the things that a sewing machine is capable of doing.

Children as young as six can run a sewing machine, and they are capable of some very free and creative work. A sewing machine can be used from elementary to high school in both art and home economics classes because not only does the sewer see immediate results from the machine, but it is also just plain fun and interesting to run it and see what kinds of things develop. Sewing machines are also still relatively inexpensive as far as fiber equipment goes, and the material to keep one running—thread—is eminently affordable. It is also a piece of equipment that can be used day in and day out by a varying number of people—one machine goes a long way. If one is concerned about recycling old fabrics, creative machine work is a good way to use them. Old curtains and used denims can be wonderfully combined with other old fabrics or new fabrics.

There will be no exact patterns or recipes given for the duplication of particular projects, because this book should act primarily as a vehicle to open the mind to the possibilities of sewing machine work. The techniques covered in this book—appliqué, patchwork, drawing, and quilting—present only the tip of the iceberg; and the uses of these techniques are myriad—as embellishments and integral parts of body coverings, furniture, sculpture, upholstery, amusements and toys, hangings, awnings, sails, window covers, tents, pillows, and quilts and coverlets. The list can go on and on; anything made from fabric can be enhanced by the machine techniques covered in this book.

This book is not an attempt to supplant the traditional hand sewing methods, but to supplement them. As an extension of the hand, the sewing machine has some obvious advantages—namely that it is far faster than hand work, and it also gives a different look.

All the pieces illustrated in this book were done on conventional home zig-zag and straight stitch machines with new and recycled fabrics.

One need not be an accomplished sewer to use the sewing machine in unconventional manners, although it is necessary to be familiar with the working methods of the particular machine being used. Some of the nicest and most successful appliqués, drawings, and quilting pieces that I have seen were done by people unfamiliar with the conventional uses of the sewing machine—they used their own methods "because they didn't know it couldn't be done."

Finally, I hope that this book will open the door to new uses of the sewing machine and show it as the multidimensional tool that it is.

1 General Information

KNOW YOUR SEWING MACHINE

The first order of business when embarking on any sewing project is to know your sewing machine well. This can be done by carefully reading the instruction booklet that comes with all machines. In the booklet will be information on threading, bobbin winding, use of accessories, and the altering of tensions and feed dog. This information will be needed to do any kind of sophisticated work.

NEEDLE SELECTION

The correct needles are very important for your work. Needles of the highest quality only should be purchased, because poor **4** needles will cause no end of trouble. Check your needles to

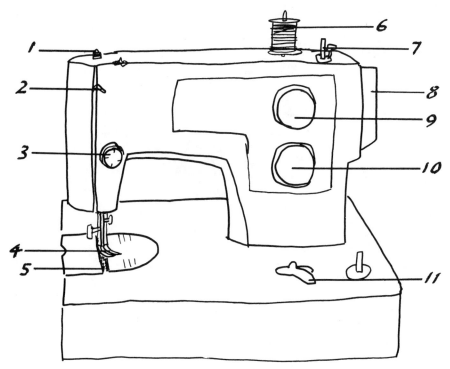

Fig. 1.1   Front view of standard home sewing machine.
Every brand of machine has the same basic parts, although
they may be in slightly different positions. (1) Presser foot
pressure regulator; (2) thread take-up lever; (3) upper thread
tension control; (4) presser foot; (5) feed dog; (6) thread spool
pins; (7) bobbin winder; (8) hand wheel; (9) control dial for
stitch width; (10) combination stitch length and reverse stitch
control; (11) feed dog control. All projects in this book
may be done on any home sewing machine.

make sure that they are not bent and that they are sharp, as a
dull or bent needle will affect the speed and general operating
ability of all machines. It is a good idea to change needles at
least once a day if you sew a great deal. Since free stitching and
quilting seem to be especially hard on needles, you should
check often to see that they have not gotten ever so slightly
bent or blunted.

The right size is also important. There are special needles for
leather and ball-point needles for knits, and these should always
be used on the appropriate materials.

5

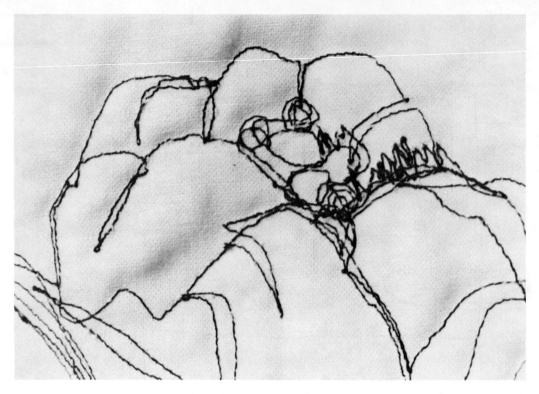

Fig. 1.2   Detail of sewing machine drawing used as quilting lines (author).

THREAD SELECTION

The appropriate thread is also important. Some people prefer polyester and some prefer cotton, but whatever the type, it should be appropriate for the job and the needle.

Generally, the thread in the bobbin should be the same size as that in the needle; however, some very interesting effects can be achieved by using a very heavy bobbin thread and a light needle thread or vice versa. The color of the thread is also important—it can blend, match, or contrast with the fabric pieces.

IRONING

An iron is an essential piece of equipment for sewing of all 6   kinds. All pieces of fabric should be ironed at the outset, and

THREAD AND NEEDLE SELECTION CHART

Thread	Needle Size	Fabric
Cotton, size 80-100	9	Fine fabrics, chiffon, net nylon
Cotton, size 80-100	11	Taffeta, light-weight medium fabrics, lace, satin, organdy.
Cotton, size 60-80 Synthetic } 50-60 Mercerized	14	Medium-weight fabrics, cotton, kettle cloth, kid leather, light wool, vinyl, velveteen, gingham, indian head.
Cotton, size 40-60 Mercerized 50 Heavy duty mercerized	16	Heavy-weight fabrics, corduroy, denim, wool coating and suiting, quilted fabrics.
Cotton, size 30-50 Heavy duty mercerized	18	Coatings, very heavy-weight fabrics, pieces like appliqués with many layers; coatings, denim.

they should be ironed periodically as the work progresses. When the work is completed, it should be given a good steam pressing.

DESIGN SELECTION

Whole books have been written on pattern and design, and since this book is concerned with techniques, mention will be made of only a few possibilities. The contents of a cupboard present a feast of visual material—labels on cans and bottles, the patterns of olives in jars, and the wonders that are found on the boxes of breakfast cereal. There is a wealth of pattern on dishes and silverware. There are many books on design in nature—every-

Fig. 1.3 Debbie Wilson examining fabric appliqué pieces in her banner *Woman at Piano*. All pieces have been sewn down, and piece is ready for lining. This large banner of different kinds of cotton fabric is made to be seen from afar, and the designer has worked up a strong dark and light statement with few small pattern areas.

Fig. 1.4 Appliqué piece, nearly completed. Sewing machine drawn details done with zig-zag stitch (Debbie Wilson).

thing from electronic microscope photographs to plant structures and sea shells, to great landscape vistas. Every public library has a fine collection of books on photography, the fine arts, and the design motifs of ancient peoples. The most important things are that the design or pattern chosen pleases the sewer and that the design is suited to the project at hand. If you are going to spend a great deal of time and effort on something, it should be something you believe worthwhile.

FABRIC SELECTION

The wonderful array of fabrics available in fabric stores today is dazzling. Whether figured or plain, they differ delightfully in texture and color. Thrift shops and second-hand stores are also good sources of fabric, as are used draperies and clothing. Sometimes these are especially nice because they have patterns that were popular ten to thirty years ago and are now no longer available. Almost any good-quality fabrics will do, but the following are a few guidelines that will save time and effort.

1. For base or background fabrics in appliqué and for patchwork pieces, a closely woven cotton, wool, or satin is best. Knits and double knits should be avoided because of their tendency to stretch. They should also be avoided for drawing or quilting because of the same tendency.

2. High-pile fabrics are not suitable for sewing machine drawings because the drawn lines get lost in the pile.

3. If an appliqué piece is to have many layers of fabric, it is best that they be layers of light-weight fabric, because the machine will not sew through many heavy layers of fabric.

If a piece of work has been used and washed (quilt, garment, etc.), the fabric should be preshrunk before work is begun.

It is important to keep in mind the use of the finished product when purchasing the fabric. If you want a washable quilt, you should choose a washable fabric; and if you want a sensuous textural interplay, you should choose fabrics such as velvet and satin.

BASTING OR PINNING

In appliqué, patchwork, or quilting, the pieces should be well pinned or basted so that they do not shift positions while the work is in progress.

TRANSFERRING YOUR DESIGN TO FABRIC

There are many methods for transferring your designs to fabric.

1. The grid method (Fig. 1.5), in which you enlarge or reduce your design;

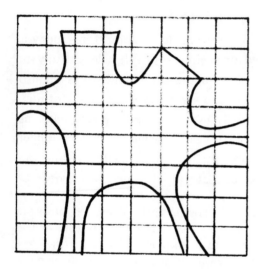

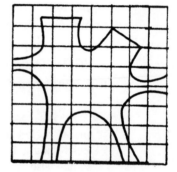

Fig. 1.5 Grid drawn to reduce or enlarge designs—the same number of squares are used, and they are proportionally larger or smaller. You can see that the same lines occur in each square, and you can enlarge or reduce the design by reproducing it square by square.

2. the photostat method of having your design photostated and then cutting it apart to use as a pattern;

3. the commercial enlarging method (most companies that photostat designs will also enlarge them);

4. the drawing method (you draw right on your fabric with pencil or dressmaker's carbon and then cut out the pieces);

5. the direct method (you cut your pieces directly out of fabric with no pattern at all).

BASIC EQUIPMENT

Sewing machine, scissors, thread, needles, fabric, tracing paper, pins, pencil, and seam ripper.

10

2 Appliqué and Patchwork

"Appliqué" comes from the French verb "to put on" or "to apply"; in terms of fabric work it simply means to attach fabric shapes to a background by means of stitches. The pieces can be sewn to the background with randomly stitched designs or with stitches following the outlines of the fabric pieces. Appliqué is one of the oldest ways of decorating cloth, and it is also one of the easiest. Found in the needlework of almost all cultures, it was and is used for many purposes—garments, quilts, and furnishing fabrics, to name just a few. In the Middle Ages it was even used as a less expensive substitute for tapestry and embroidery.

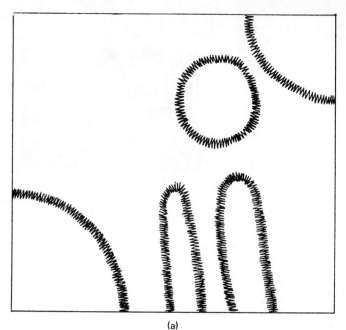

(a)

Fig. 2.1 (a) Illustration of one appliqué method using only zig-zag stitches to attach fabric. (b) Appliqué method using zig-zag and straight stitches to attach fabric.

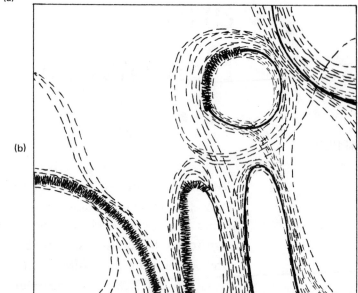

(b)

PATCHWORK

"Patchwork" and "piecework" have come to mean the same thing in our vernacular. Both mean a mosaic of pieces of fabric seamed together edge to edge to make a larger piece of fabric.

12

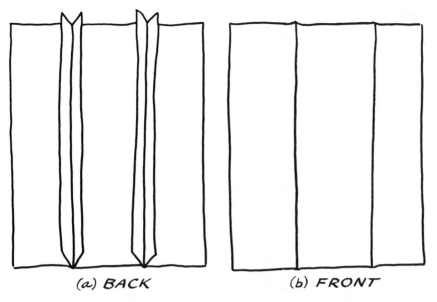

(a) BACK   (b) FRONT

Fig. 2.2 (a) Back of patchwork piece. It can be seen that the
fabric pieces are put together edge-to-edge and sewn on the
wrong or back side. (b) Front of patchwork piece. It can
be seen that there are no stitches visible on the
front side.

This can be done with simple shapes such as strips or squares or
with more intricate shapes like hexagons. Probably originally
developed to make use of small scraps of fabric (as in early
American patchwork quilts) and for the decorative repair of
garments and household fabrics, it is much used now as a design
entity in itself.

The sewing machine can cut down tremendously on the time
needed to complete both appliqué and patchwork, and it can
achieve effects that are not possible when these techniques are
done by hand. The machine has added a new vocabulary of
possibilities to these very ancient technique.

SEWING MACHINE APPLIQUÉ

METHOD # 1

The appliqué method most easily done by sewing machine
requires a zig-zag machine or a machine with a zig-zag
13 attachment.

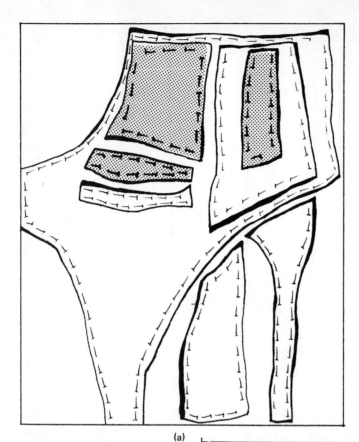

(a)

Fig. 2.3 (a) Diagram of appliqué in progress—many smaller fabric pieces laid on and pinned to fabric background. (b) Closeup of appliqué piece—part of fabric appliqué design sewn on to background with close-together zig-zag stitch. It can be seen that the zig-zag stitches cover up the raw edges.

(b)

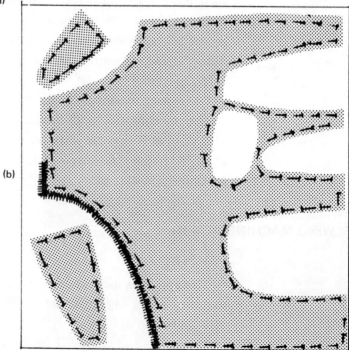

14

The appliqué itself can take any form—you do or redo a painting or photograph, a collage, assemblage, or a simple geometric design. You can use all new fabric, all old fabric, or a combination of both. (The fabric should, however, be of a good quality.) There are absolutely no definite rules. You should remember that running a sewing machine is fun, and this kind of work should be enjoyable and interesting. The finished product can be used for anything where a fabric piece would be appropriate.

1. Once you have decided on a design, you should transfer your design to full size to brown paper. (Newspaper can be used to get the design shapes, but it should not be used for this step because of the tendency of the ink to rub off onto fabrics.)

2. The brown paper pattern should then be cut apart and the pieces used just as you would use used pieces of a dress pattern—i.e., put on the fabric and the fabric pieces cut out. These fabric pieces, which are the appliqué pieces, should be cut exactly to size with no seam allowance.

3. These appliqué pieces will now be pinned or basted to the background fabric, with the grain lines of the appliqué pieces and of the background running in the same direction. This will prevent most, but not all, of the puckering which happens when fabric is laid on fabric. If the appliqué pieces are put onto the background on the bias, a bubble effect will result, which in some cases could add to the design. Especially if small areas are going to be stuffed, a bias piece will allow the fabric to stretch to accommodate the stuffing. When one shape overlaps another, lay the bottom one down first. When you are sewing them down, you can put the bottom or first layer of shapes down and sew them on, and then go to the next layer and sew them on, proceeding in this manner until all the pieces are sewn down, or you can pin or baste all the shapes down at once and sew them all down at one time. It makes no difference.

4. Set the sewing machine on the closest together zig-zag stitch following all the directions in the instruction booklet for tension setting. Special care should be given here to the selection of the thread color, since the stitching will itself become a very important part of the design. The thread color can blend with the color of the appliqué pieces, contrast with them, or be a color such as black or navy blue, which will make the colors of the individual pieces appear brighter.

5. Stitch down all the appliqué pieces along the edges, making sure that the stitches cover all the raw edges. (The fact that the zig-zag stitches cover the raw edges is what makes it possible to cut all the appliqué shapes to size and not allow an extra margin for seams or hem.) The sewing down of the appliqué shapes should be a fairly rapid

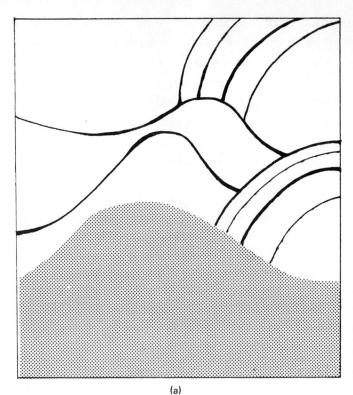

(a)

Fig. 2.4 Placement of appliqué pieces. (a) Top layers placed *over* bottom layers and (b) ends of bottom layers that are overlapped can remain with raw edges and do not have to be sewn.

(b)

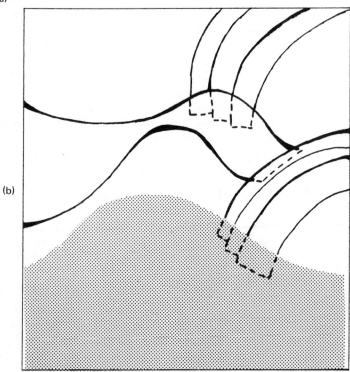

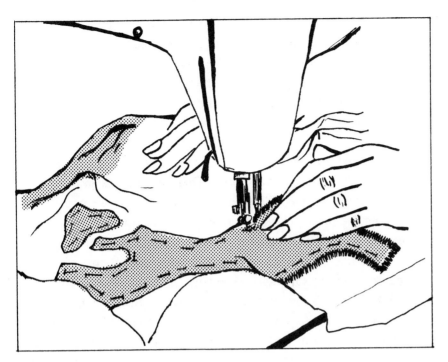

Fig. 2.5 Zig-zag appliqué piece in progress. Hands are guiding
the fabric along. This is the best placement of the hands to
guide fabric along curving lines.

process. This technique makes a very strong fabric piece which can
stand much wear. The machine stitches give a clean, crisp look to the
appliqué piece. In the late nineteenth century the same effect was
achieved by the very slow process of covering the raw edges with
closely spaced hand-done satin or buttonhole stitches.

6. Appliqué pieces should be finished according to their use. If a
piece is going to be a hanging, it can be stretched over a canvas
stretcher, or if it is going to hang free like a banner, it can be lined with
any appropriate lining fabric and weighted in the bottom with drapery
weight.

METHOD #2

This second method of sewing machine appliqué is especially
effective when you want to work up textural areas. It is the
same as the first method except for the manner in which the
appliqué pieces are sewn on. In this method, both straight and
zig-zag stitches are used, and the stitches not only follow the
outline of the individual pieces, but they also run along the
background and make rich patterns within the appliqué pieces.

17

These two methods can be used together, and any other method of attaching fabric to background by machine is a viable method of sewing machine appliqué. Hand detailing of all kinds can, of course, be used with either method.

In the quilt illustrated in Figure 2.6, "Happy Birthday, America," all of the images and letter forms were appliquéd on square patches of permanent-press fabric. The patches were constructed and moved around from place to place until a pleasing arrangement was found. There was no design to follow, but merely an idea of using American symbols to create a rectangular piece. Working "freestyle" like this is an interesting way to work and allows for a great deal of spontaneity. It can be seen that the blocks are not all the same shape—some are square, some rectangular, some large, and some small. The focal point of the design is the George Washington portrait in the center; the design was worked out from the center to all four sides. It is a good idea to keep in mind that appliqué pieces are enhanced by a combination of fabrics and textures and by the repetition of shapes in color and size. In the "Happy Birthday" quilt there are, in addition to the permanent-press fabrics, metallic fabrics, ribbons, military medals, and satin fabrics. The stripes and stars, which appear throughout the quilt in different areas, serve to hold the whole design together. The sewing machine drawings of buffalo nickels, on either side of the center, also serve to unite the design. The stripes and the x-designs at the upper end were done in the patchwork technique. After all the blocks were completed, they were pinned together in large sections—top, bottom, right side, left side—and the whole thing was stitched together in the patchwork method. To finish, a dacron batting was pinned to the top, the piece was lined with a cotton lining, and the entire piece was quilted with a straight sewing machine stitch along the lines formed by the edges of the individual patches.

The use of transparent fabrics to build up rich color areas is illustrated in Figure 2.7, "What's a nice girl like you doing in a place like this?" by Jeannie Ilgen. The artist has achieved very subtle darks and lights and color areas by the use of the organdy, organza, and net. After the underlayers were sewn

Fig. 2.6 *Happy Birthday, America.* Appliqué quilt with drawing and patchwork. Cotton, satin, metallic fabrics, and needlepoint (author).

Fig. 2.7 *"What's a nice girl like you doing in a place like this?"*
Appliqué using layers of transparent fabrics (Jeannie Ilgen).

down in segments, one overlay of very transparent fabric was put down over the whole area to tie it together. (Often a little spray starch should be sprayed on very light fabrics to give them extra body and make them move through the feed dog easier.) This technique of using transparent fabrics is good also if you have put too many colors down and they appear too brilliant or garish. An overlay of a transparent fabric will cut down both the intensity of the colors and the value contrast. Jeannie used a photograph as the design source and took it to a blueprint company to have it enlarged. This enlargement was cut apart to be used as the pattern. In this case it was cut apart according to the dark and light areas. The facial features were drawn with the sewing machine drawing technique that will be discussed in

20

Chapter Three. The stark black background in this piece contributes to the mood of the piece and makes the figure with all the subtleties of color stand out.

Embellishing existing garments has great possibilities for appliqué and other kind of decorative stitching. In the jeans by Sally Kinsey, in Figures 2.8 and 2.9, you can see the use of appliqué methods number one and number two. You can also see the decorative possibilities of the zig-zag stitches by themselves and their use in relation to the appliqué patches. The materials used are from many sources—new fabrics, old fabrics, clothing labels, pieces of old laces and doilies, and braids and trims. The patches and appliqué pieces were placed in a random fashion and sewn in the same way—with the stitches sometimes following the perimeter of the appliqué pieces and sometimes

Fig. 2.8 Appliqué on blue jeans—back of jeans (Sally Kinsey).

Fig. 2.9 Appliqué on jeans—detail
(Sally Kinsey).

crossing from the interior of the patches to the background. The look of the appliqué pieces is quite handsome when they are attached in this manner. This would also be a good technique to use for larger hanging or garment pieces where the interplay of textural areas is important. Figures 2.10 and 2.11 are also by Sally Kinsey, and are of a more experimental type. Figure 2.10 shows appliqué on wide satin ribbon. Many pieces of this ribbon were sewn together to form a larger piece of fabric. The patch in Figure 2.11, again a small piece meant to be incorporated into a larger piece, shows not only the use of the zig-zag stitch to attach the pieces, but also the use of all of the ends of the threads to form a linear design element on the surface. Figure 2.12 shows some further experiments by Sally, **22** stitched ribbons both flat and stuffed to form a neckpiece held

Fig. 2.10 Appliqué on satin ribbon—detail (Sally Kinsey).

Fig. 2.11 Experimental piece. Excess threads form part of the pattern (Sally Kinsey).

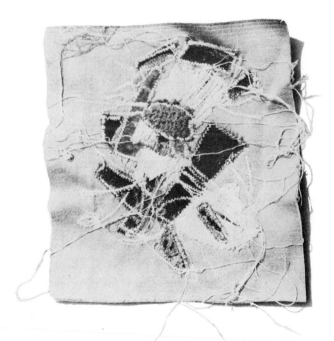

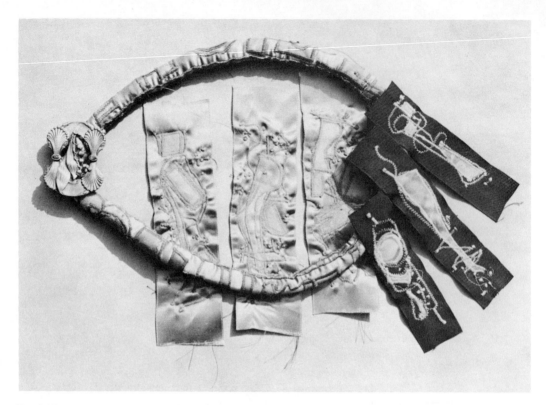

Fig. 2.12 Neckpiece in progress—appliqué on satin and
grosgrain ribbons. Neckpiece held together with Victorian pin
(Sally Kinsey).

together with a Victorian brass pin. Figure 2.13, a neckpiece in
progress, again by Sally Kinsey, is stitched on an old pant leg.
Both the front and the back of the leg are used, which gives a
very firm foundation. The zig-zag stitches not only cover the
raw edges of the fabric, but also cut in and around the patches
to form a secondary linear pattern. Again, you can see the use
of fabric with many different textures and how successfully
they all work together.

In the "T.S. Eliot" quilt, Figure 2.14, the use of tie-dyed
fabric as a design element can be seen. Again, this piece is
created from many different shaped patches sewn together. This
quilt uses fabrics of many different origins—tie-dyed fabric,
needlepoint, homespun, satin, velvet, and taffeta. The individual
blocks are quite different in subject matter and technique, but
the colors of the quilt—blues, greens, purples, and golds—serve

24 to bring the composition together. The detail, in Figure 2.15,

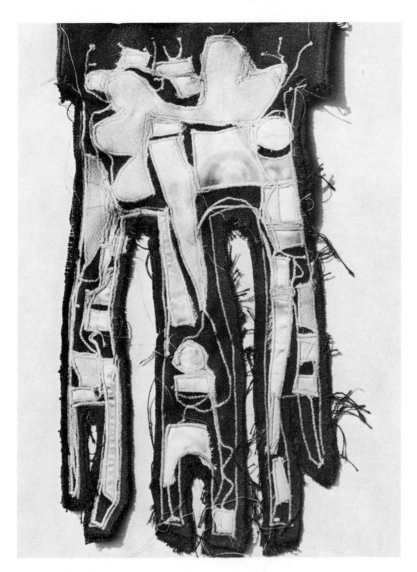

Fig. 2.13 Neckpiece in progress—appliqué on pant leg (Sally Kinsey).

shows a figure for which the pieces were cut very quickly and left unrefined. Its spontaneous look contrasts nicely with the designs in the rest of the quilt block. In another detail, Figure 2.16, there is an extra row of stitches around one of the figures which was made to work like a Mach line in television. (This was done in a complementary color to the stitching around the figure.)

25

Fig. 2.14 *T.S. Eliot Quilt.* Cotton, wool, tie-dyed corduroy;
appliqué and patchwork (author).

Fig. 2.15 *T.S. Eliot Quilt.* Appliqué—detail.

Fig. 2.16 *T.S. Eliot Quilt.* Appliqué
and patchwork—detail.

The quilt patches in Figures 2.17 through 2.26 illustrate many appliqué techniques, from straight appliqué with the close zig-zag to reembroidering the fabric and stuffing it, to working up color areas through transparency. These quilt blocks were all done by students in my classes and given to me to make up a quilt from each class. This has proven to be an excellent way to remember each student who crosses my path—a nice contemporary adaptation of the old friendship quilt idea. These blocks are easy to sew together because of their uniform size, 15″ X 15″.

Fig. 2.17

Fig. 2.18

Fig. 2.19

Fig. 2.20

Fig. 2.21

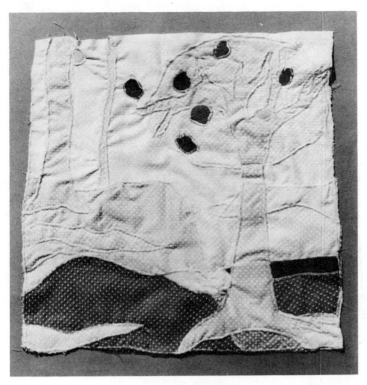

Fig. 2.22

Fig. 2.23

Fig. 2.24

Fig. 2.25

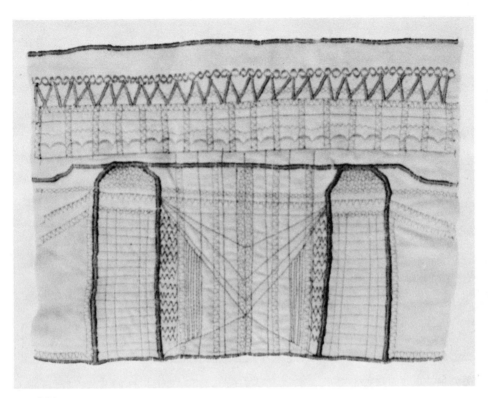

Fig. 2.26

Figures 2.27, 2.28, 2.29, and 2.30 are illustrations of liturgical appliqué pieces that were done by students in my experimental textiles class for the campus chapel. (They were done on a commission basis so that the students could learn how to work on a commission and so that the chapel could be decorated with student works.) Liturgical banners and vestments lend themselves very well to modern appliqué methods, and appliqué pieces not only look beautiful but are very serviceable for church or synagogue use. They can be crafted by one person or a committee. Figure 2.27 shows a vestment by Albert Sardelli in satin and velvets. The front and back flame motifs were appliquéd onto the background with fabrics of different textures; and the appliqué pieces were slit along the underside, stuffed, and resewn. This allows them to stand out in relief from the satin background.

Figure 2.28, an appliqué piece with a quilted form, is a
33 balcony hanging by Susan Point. The stuffed area is the circular

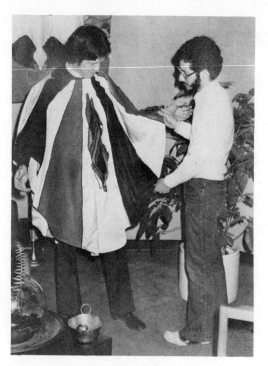

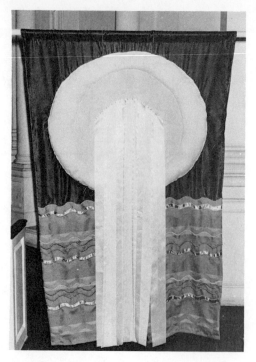

Fig. 2.27 Albert Sardelli—liturgical vestment. Satin and velvet. Albert adjusting the fit on Paul Bosch (collection of Hendricks Chapel; photo by Syracuse University News Bureau).

Fig. 2.28 Susan Point—liturgical banner. Cotton, satin, and satin ribbon (collection of Hendricks Chapel; photo by Syracuse University News Bureau).

form in the center. The ribbons that hang from the center are sewn only at the top so that they can move in the breeze as the doors of the chapel are opened and closed. It is interesting to note that the artist made the appliqué shapes at the bottom echo the shapes in the printed background fabric. Printed fabrics should not be overlooked in appliqué because appliqué pieces can enhance or add to the printed fabric. These bottom appliqué shapes on Susan's piece are satin, and a nice textural interplay occurs between the cotton background and the appliqué. Figure 2.29, a banner by Cathy Canfield, was done for the main office of the chapel. Here the artist has used symbols for many of the world's major religions as her theme and organized them in an eight-pointed star so that the small symbols are not lost on the background. You can see that there **34** is a strong pattern in the circle and star which can be seen from

Fig. 2.29 Cathy Canfield—Satin, cotton, and velvet appliqué
banner done for Hendricks Chapel office. Appliqué depicts
symbols for religions of the world (collection of Hendricks
Chapel; photo by Syracuse University News Bureau).

Fig. 2.30 Five altar and pulpit falls (Joann Oguro and Janice Keaveney; collection of Hendricks Chapel; photo by Syracuse University News Bureau).

afar, even before the individual symbols are discerned. Figure 2.30, a series of pulpit and altar falls by Janice Keaveney and Joann Oguro, are also made to be seen from a distance and there is a simple breakup of the space so that they, too, read as a graphic statement when viewed from the back of the chapel. There are also many color and textural changes in the fabrics used, but the symbols themselves are as simplified as possible. Figures 2.31 and 2.32 (detail), "Apotheosis of Marilyn Monroe," by the author is an appliqué and patchwork piece with a needlepoint insert. The fabrics used are felt, cotton, and antique satin. The same seated-woman image was used five times, each time differently, with a different color fabric and thread and with a different negative-positive orientation. In the detail it can be seen once more how nicely the zig-zag stitches cover the raw edges.

36

Fig. 2.31 *Apotheosis of Marilyn Monroe.* Appliqué and
patchwork hanging. Wool, felt, cotton, and polyester with
needlepoint insert (author).

Fig. 2.32 *Apotheosis of Marilyn Monroe.*
Detail.

Figure 2.33, Louise Pietrafesa's "Homage to M & M's" is an appliqué and quilted piece 6 feet long and made to be used as a seating unit or furniture piece. It is done in brushed corduroy with the lettering appliquéd on with the zig-zag stitch and the thin letters drawn on with the zig-zag stitch. It is washable and able to withstand much wear because of the strength of both the fabrics and the stitching. The ends of the "package" are quilted, and it is backed with the same fabric. It is stuffed with many little round satin and taffeta "M & M" candy pillows which can be easily removed (to make the piece appear less stuffed) by means of a long upholstery zipper at one end. It is a very comfortable and novel idea for a seating unit, bringing to mind additional possibilities using items from the candy store and the kitchen cupboard. Figures 2.34 and 2.35,

Fig. 2.33 *Homage to M & M's.* Soft couch with 100 M & M pillows. Piece is 6 feet long. It is usually stuffed with all of the little pillows (Louise Pietrafesa).

details of the author's "Giant Bird Quilt," illustrate a child's quilt with many bird forms cut from fabric scraps—the scraps that fell from cut-out pieces. There is almost no way to go wrong when using scrap pieces like that because they come in infinite varieties of shape, size, and color. They are not difficult to put together in whimsical and funny bird shapes. Since the quilt was made for a child, many textural differences in the fabrics were used so that there will be many tactile sensations.

There are also small open places under wings and beaks where little hands can explore. My little boy gets great delight from looking at and feeling this quilt. Qualities other than strictly visual ones can be worked into appliqué pieces. As already mentioned, the tactile quality plays a big part in quilts and garments, and they almost beg to be touched. I often put petals or cloves or powder sachet into appliqué pieces to delight the nose. One of my fondest memories is of a teddy bear with a bell in his ear, and when I make pieces for children I often include

39

Fig. 2.34 *Giant Bird Quilt.* Wool, felt, cotton, and ribbon pieces (author).

little bells or other sound-makers to stimulate the sense of hearing.

Figure 2.36 and Figures 2.37 to 2.40 show Laurene Piston's quilt of butterflies and bugs. Done in washable cottons this quilt reflects her husband's interest in entymology. The insect shapes vary in size, and all are in the green, blue, brown, and purple color range. They are based on examples from zoology

40

Fig. 2.35 *Giant Bird Quilt.* Detail.

Fig. 2.36 *Bug Quilt.* Appliqué and quilting (Laurene Piston).

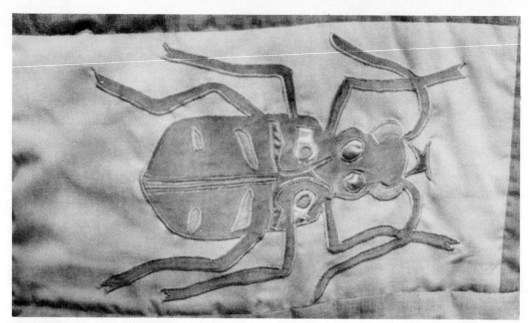

Fig. 2.37

Fig. 2.38

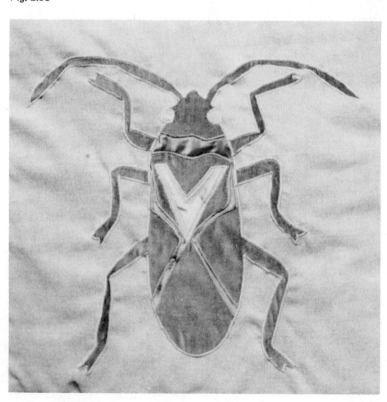

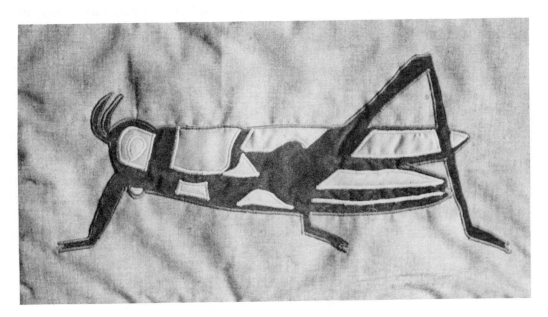

Fig. 2.39

Fig. 2.40

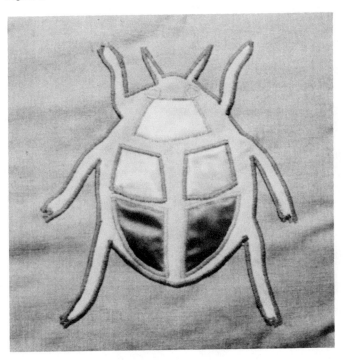

books. Books of science and related areas supply further sources of inspiration. Biology, zoology, shells, and herbs are just a few illustratable topics. The basic cell structures of plants, animals, and minerals can be of great beauty, and they are often suitable as the point of departure for appliqué forms.

Toys and amusements of all kinds are other forms that can be embellished with appliqué pieces. Figure 2.41 shows the front

Fig. 2.41 Front appliqué piece for sorcerer doll (unfinished).
Cotton and satin (author).

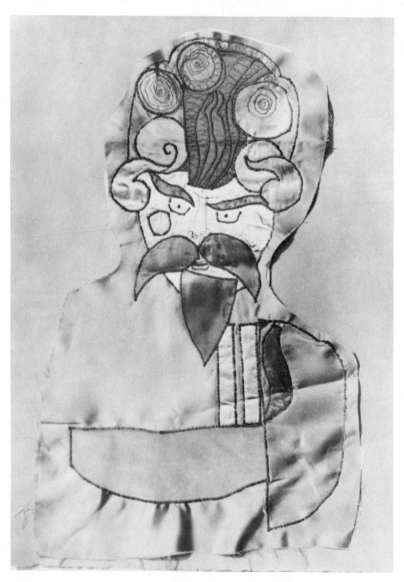

of an unfinished sorcerer doll with large appliqué pieces and sewing machine-drawn details. This will be a toy for a very young child when it is completed, and it will be backed with a plain piece of satin, filled with dacron stuffing, and scented with lavender. You can see that the shape will be simple for a child to handle and that its attractiveness is due to the appliqué pieces. There need be no buttons or beads for the child to swallow. Figures 2.42 and 2.43 are details of two experimental pieces by Alyse McNeely Sharoff. Alyse used frayed fabric and heavy yarns couched down. Some of the yarns which are couched down with the zig-zag stitch have ceramic discs attached to the ends. The use of varying lengths and widths of zig-zag stitches can also be seen. (Since both the zig-zag and straight stitches have many inherent variations, you should endeavor to take advantage of these variations.) These examples show that almost any method you use to attach one piece of fabric to another and any kind of fabric or material you use is perfectly acceptable for sewing machine appliqué.

Plate 11, "Lady in Hat" by Jean Henry, is a large appliqué piece stretched over canvas stretchers. It uses much recycled fabric—terrycloth for the background and old brocade curtains

Fig. 2.42 Experimental piece—appliqué and fraying (Alyse McNeely Sharoff).

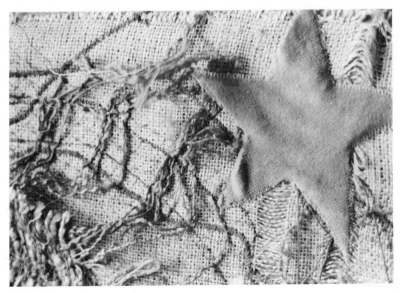

Fig. 2.43 Experimental piece—appliqué and fraying with ceramic beads (Alyse McNeely Sharoff).

from the forties for the woman's dress. All the detail work is drawn on with the zig-zag and straight stitches of sewing machines. Plate 5, "Policemen" by Alyse McNeely Sharoff (see color insert), is also a large appliqué stretched over canvas stretchers. In this piece a very nice dark and light, negative-positive pattern is arrived at by the use of the simple shapes of the men against the background. All the details are drawn in with the sewing machine drawing technique. The fabrics are wool and cotton, and the fabrics have been pieced in the patchwork technique to get the large dark shapes. The patchwork quilt top, Figure 2.44, was done in New Hampshire in the 1930s. It is sewn together in the patchwork technique, fabric edge to fabric edge. All the pieces have straight edges. This is the easiest way to do patchwork, because you cannot ease the fabric in sufficiently to patch curved shapes.

Fig. 2.44 Sewing machine patchwork—cotton fabrics. Made in
1930s in New Hampshire (collection of the author).

3 Drawing

Stop! Before you quickly turn this page and flip through this chapter with that old cliché, "I can't draw a straight line," on your lips, read the pages through, look at the diagrams, and see just what a fun, marvelous, and easy drawing tool the sewing machine is.

The sewing machine draws with a wonderful, free, loose quality that is almost impossible to get with other instruments. Those loose and free lines you get (because the sewing machine sews in its particular way) make it almost impossible not to do a sucessful piece. Whatever your product comes out to be, it will be a right and correct piece of work.

Sewn drawings can be used for a myriad of purposes—when you want to have drawn images or linear patterns as a part of a piece of work. Sewn drawings are far superior to pen or paint **48** lines—not only because of their attractive looks, but also because they are a textile technique and can be cared for (washed, ironed) along with the rest of the piece. They are also quicker to execute than hand-embroidered drawings. Sewn drawings can be used as drawings which stand on their own as drawings, and they are marvelous as detailing on appliqué of quilted pieces. They can be used to accentuate the design on printed fabrics, to add such things as features and details on dolls and toys of all kinds, and can be put on garments before or after they are finished. Sewn drawings can be put on hangings, pillows, furniture, and just anywhere you would put sewing or appliqué.

There is *no* "wrong way" to do sewing machine drawings! They have a wonderful serendipity about them no matter what you draw or how you guide your machine when you draw—even if you just move your fabric back and forth under the needle.

Sewing machine drawings are fun, interesting, and challenging to do, and the following steps should make the process easily understandable.

FABRIC CHOICES

Although theoretically this technique can be done on any fabric, some materials work better than others. The best choices for fabrics are closely woven cottons and cotton blends, satins, taffetas, and light wools including felts. This technique does not work particularly well on knits and double knits, high pile fabrics such as corduroy, velvet, and fake furs. (The pile on these fabrics hides the sewing.)

Step 1. Put the feed dog on your machine down. (There should be a knob for this on your machine.)

Step 2. Loosen the pressure on your presser foot. (Note that steps 1 and 2 are the same as the directions for "darning" in most sewing machine books.)

Step 3. Check the sharpness of the needle, since a sharp needle is imperative for drawings.

Step 4. Check the thread tension. It should be set for the particular kind of fabric you are using.

Step 5. Set stitch length at medium stitch.

There are three possibilities for the next step. Pick one of them:

Step 6a (see Fig. 3.1). Do a loose drawing, or make guidelines of any kind on the side of the fabric facing the presser foot (facing up). This should be done with a pencil or some kind of dressmaker's carbon, to allow the guidelines to be washed off or erased and also to prevent them from running if they are washed. (Do not use felt-tip pens or ballpoints for the same reasons.) Put the fabric under the presser foot.

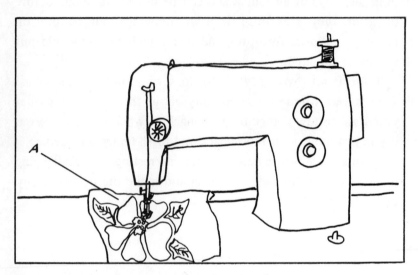

Fig. 3.1   Pencil or carbon drawing (A) on fabric. The drawing is facing up toward the pressure foot. This will be the *wrong* side of the drawing. The bobbin side or underside will be the right side of the drawing.

Step 6b (see Fig. 3.2). Insert the fabric under the presser foot with no guidelines or preliminary drawings. With this method you compose your drawing at the time of sewing.

Step 6c (see Fig. 3.3). Do a drawing on tracing paper. Put the tracing paper on top of the fabric and insert the fabric with the tracing paper on top under the presser foot.

Step 7. Put the presser foot down, just as you would for all normal sewing. (This is most important, since putting the presser foot down controls the thread tension and keeps the fabric in place.)

Step 8. You are now ready to begin the drawing process. Start the machine, and move the fabric in all directions (right, left, forward and backward) according to your plans, pre-sketched or spontaneous. When you're moving the fabric, do it fast sometimes and slowly other times, as this will give you stitches of different lengths. Also, try to sew over the same sewn lines over and over. This not only builds up light and

Plate 1
Happy Birthday, America
Quilting, appliqué, drawing,
patchwork (author)

Plate 2
Happy Birthday, America
Detail (author)

Plate 3
Forms
Drawing, appliqué (Peggy Mendes)

Plate 4
Medusa
Quilted form (Nancy Trimble)

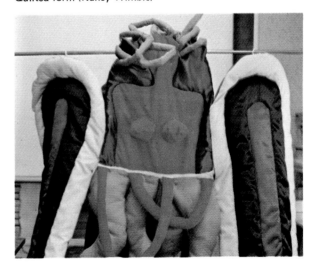

Plate 5
Policemen
Appliqué and drawing
(Alyse McNeely Sharoff)

Plate 6
Syracuse University Scene
Transparent appliqué on window frame
(Karen Richards)

Plate 7
Sleeping Bag
Patchwork and quilting (Harriete Berman)

Plate 8
The Kiss
Appliqué and drawing (Jean Henry)

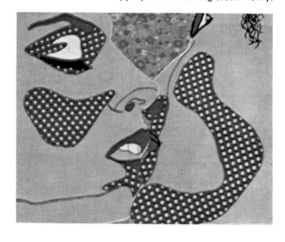

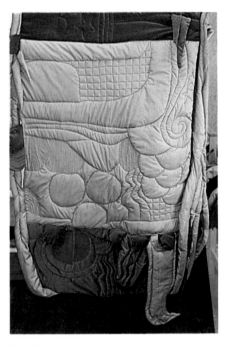

Plate 9
Quilted Form
Quilting (Nancy Trimble)

Plate 10
Decade-Spanning, Mind-Expanding,
Star-Studded Wonder
Quilting, appliqué, patchwork; collection
Everson Museum of Art, Syracuse, N. Y.
(author)

Plate 11
Lady in Hat
Appliqué and drawing (Jean Henry)

Plate 12
Shield
Appliqué (Buffy Point)

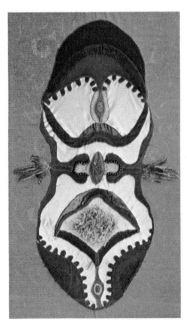

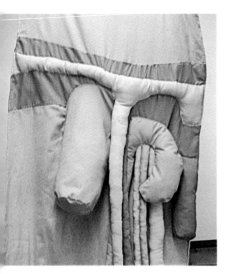

Plate 13
Quilt with Arms
Quilting and patchwork
(Hope W. Sylvester)

Plate 14
Husky
Appliqué (student work)

Plate 15
Freud and Anna Freud
Appliqué and drawing (Nancy Trimble)

Plate 16
Anna Freud
Detail (Nancy Trimble)

Plate 17
Apotheosis of Marilyn Monroe
Appliqué and patchwork
with needlepoint insert (author)

Plate 18
Botanical Print (quilt patch)
Appliqué and drawing (Lois Karlin)

Plate 19
Fiancé
Appliqué and drawing
(Alyse McNeely Sharoff)

Plate 20
Flapper
Appliqué and drawing (Cathy Canfield)

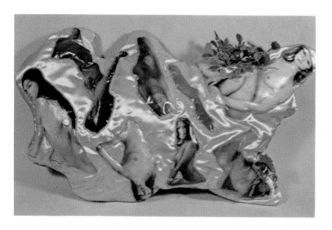

Plate 21
Cut Out Quilt
Appliqué and quilting (Harriete Berman)

Plate 22
Artichoke Wingtip
Appliqué and patchwork
(Hope W. Sylvester)

Plate 23
T. S. Eliot Quilt
Appliqué, patchwork, drawing,
and quilting (author)

Plate 24
T. S. Eliot Quilt
Detail (author)

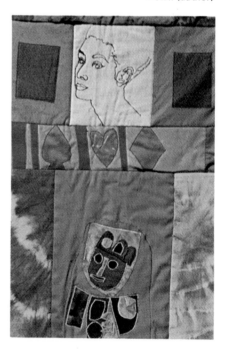

Plate 25
Quilt with Japanese Motifs
Appliqué, patchwork, and quilting
(Joann Oguro)

Plate 26
Giant Bird Quilt
Detail; appliqué, patchwork, and quilting
(author)

Plate 27
Lady Bugs
Appliqué (Lois Moore)

Plate 28
Landscape
Drawing on halter of dress (Susanne Gee)

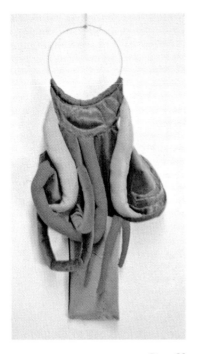

Plate 29
Quilted Body Covering
Quilting (Nancy Trimble)

Plate 30
Face
Appliqué (Alice Rich)

Plate 31
Panel
Appliqué (Sue Fager)

Plate 32
Egg Piece
Appliqué and quilting
(Alyse McNeely Sharoff)

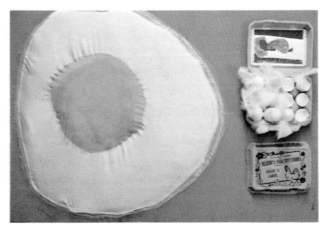

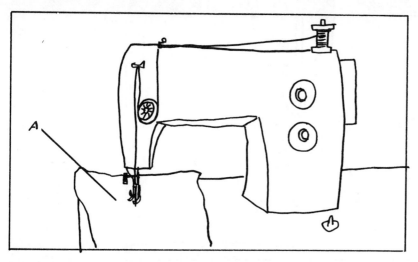

Fig. 3.2 Drawing (A) ready to be done with *no* guidelines.
In this case either needle side or bobbin side could be right
side.

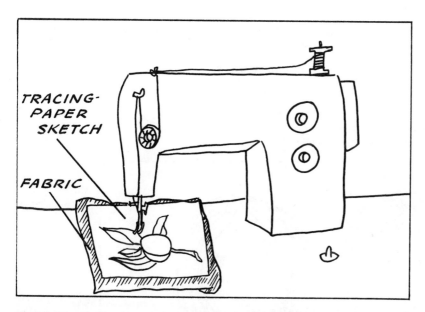

Fig. 3.3 Diagram showing use of tracing-paper sketch laid over
fabric. The sewing is done over the sketch, the tracing paper
sketch is ripped away, and the bobbin side of the fabric is
the right side.

dark areas, but also builds up pleasing textural qualities. If you wish to
go from one area of the drawing to another, pull the needle up, move
the fabric to a new area, put the needle down, and continue sewing (see
Fig. 3.4). When you do this, there will be floating threads on both the

51

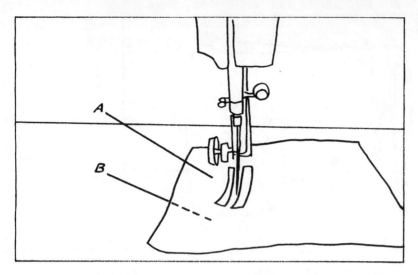

Fig. 3.4   Diagram showing needle side of drawing (A) facing
up, and bobbin side of drawing (B) facing down.

top and bottom of the piece. These can be easily cut off at the completion of the piece.

Step 9. Remove the sewn drawing from under the presser foot and iron it.

Fig. 3.5   (a) Floating threads on the surface caused by lifting
needle; (b) the same drawing with floating threads cut.

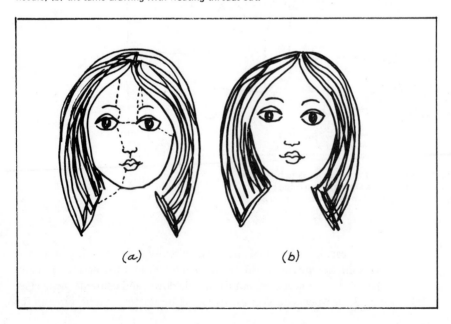

Depending on which method you use at Step 6, you will have a different right side to your drawing. With Step 6a the right side of your drawing will be the under or bobbin side of the fabric (as you will not want the guidelines to be seen). With Step 6b either side of the fabric, the top or the bobbin side, can be the right side because you have no guidelines to hide. With Step 6c you will need to rip away the tracing paper, after which either side can be the right side.

You will notice that the bobbin side of the fabric has marvelous loops and loose stitches which are usually thought of as "bad" in other sewing, but which add a wonderful textural look to your sewn drawing.

A word should be inserted here on the use of the embroidery hoop for free stitching and sewn drawings. I have found that it is hard to manipulate the fabric and see what is being done when the fabric is in a hoop. The working area is also cut down severely. However, if you wish to use it, remove the presser foot, insert the fabric in the hoop, and proceed from Step 1 just as you would with the other methods.

In the series of drawings by the author (Figs. 3.6 through 3.15), you can see the use of the technique in Step 6a (where a light pencil drawing is put on the fabric, the images are sewn/drawn, and the bobbin side of the fabric is the right side of the drawings). You can see the long and short stitches and the very nice texture that is made by the loops that are formed by the bobbin thread, and you can see how the light and dark areas in the drawing are arrived at by sewing over and over the same areas. When these are sewn, the sewing machine was being run very fast so that I did not have complete control. That is what is responsible for the loose quality of these pieces. I *never* follow the sketched lines exactly—not only because it's more fun to draw using very vaguely sketched lines, but also because the finished product has a fresh and lively look instead of a labored look.

Figure 3.16, by Flora Kinsey, age 9, illustrates what can be done by a child. They are some of the best sewers and drawers possible. They do not need any guidelines, and their products are always delightful. This drawing was done over pieces of felt

Fig. 3.6 Friend—drawing (author).

Drawing

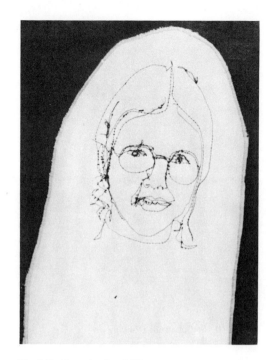

Fig. 3.8 Portrait of a child on muslin (author).

Fig. 3.9 Portrait of Pat. Drawing on muslin zig-zagged down to linen (author).

Fig. 3.7

Fig. 3.10 Self-portrait. Drawing on muslin (author).

Fig. 3.11 Friend—drawing (author).

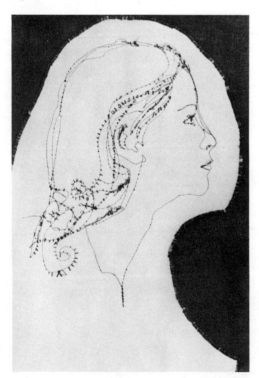

Fig. 3.12 Girl—drawing (author).

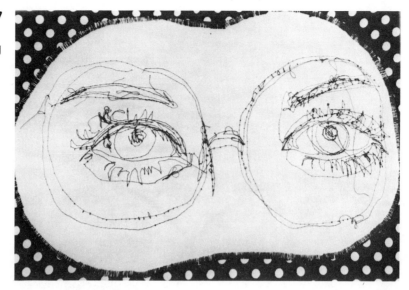

Fig. 3.13 Eyes—drawing (author).

Fig. 3.14 Girl—drawing (author).

Fig. 3.15 Girl (author).

Fig. 3.16 *Experiments* (Flora Kinsey, age 9).

Fig. 3.17   Neckpiece detail with zircon. Drawing and hand
stitching on wool felt (Pat Nelson).

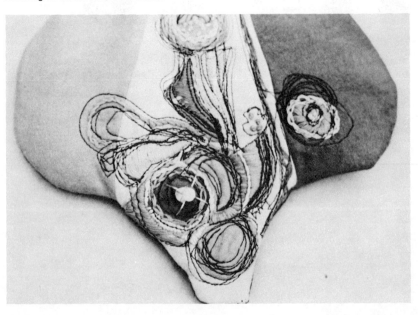

and other scraps of fabric. Figure 3.17, by Pat Nelson, is the bottom part of a fabric neckpiece. It is made of wool felt with felt appliques. The hand stitching is accented with sewing machine drawing, and the piece is set with a zircon. The machine stitching is black, which sets off the colors, accents the shapes, and gives the whole piece a free and loose look. The machine drawing on this piece was worked with the top facing up so that the machine stitching could be aligned with the hand stitching and the appliqued pieces. This piece, lined with the same wool felt, comes around the neck and buttons in the back.

Another piece of fabric jewelry is illustrated in Figures 3.18 and 3.19 (detail) by the author. This piece is an "eye" image which was drawn on a piece of white cotton fabric; the fabric was then mounted on a round piece of aluminum, set with a synthetic sapphire, and hung on a hand-made silver chain. It is a humorous piece that is always fun to wear. As the "eye" here was drawn without a pencil sketch, either side of the drawing

Fig. 3.18 Eye pendant. Drawing on cotton, stretched on metal, and set with synthetic sapphire, then hung from silver chain (author).

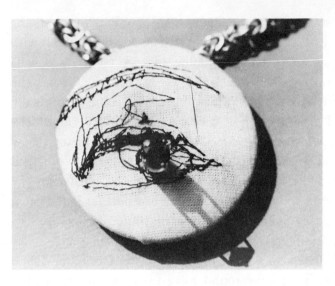

Fig. 3.19 Eye pendant. Detail—drawing on cotton, stretched on metal, and set with synthetic sapphire on silver chain (author).

could have been used as the right side. I am in the process of doing drawings on a dress to match the "eye" motifs in the jewelry. The drawings can be done all over the dress because they become as much a part of the dress as the stitches that hold it together. They need no special care in washing or ironing.

Another neckpiece by the author, Figure 3.20, is an appliqué and drawing piece in which the drawing is a random drawing. The piece was moved back and forth under the presser foot so that the stitches not only work as a drawing but also hold down the appliqué pieces. This fabric piece was stretched over a round piece of aluminum and set with a synthetic ruby on a tiffany setting. Barbara Gentry's very handsome piece, "Skaneateles," Figure 3.21, is a combination of sewing machine drawing, hand sewing, and quilting. It depicts the main street of an upstate New York village and has the look of a lithograph or a pen drawing. The individual sections were done building by building, and then the total unit was put together. The piece is done on muslin with black thread to further accentuate the look of a print. The side of the fabric seen here is the top side, or the side that was up and toward the needle. There are no loops such as one would find on the bobbin side. In the two details from the

60 "Happy Birthday, America" quilt, "George Washington" (Fig.

Fig. 3.20 Neckpiece. Random drawing set with synthetic ruby
(author).

Fig. 3.21 *Skaneateles.* Drawing on muslin combined with hand
stitching and quilting (Barbara Gentry).

3.22), and "Presidential Portraits" (Fig. 3.23), you can see sewn drawings used as parts of larger pieces. In the Washington portrait, a few features of George and a bit of patriotic ribbon are enough to say "George Washington." It can also be seen how sewing over and over an area can build up dark areas (around the eyes and the nose). Many times just a suggestion of the form is enough. The presidential portraits are also very loosely drawn with a minimum of lines. The negative areas in these drawings were painted with a very thin coat of acrylic fabric dyes. The apple appliqué, cut from a printed fabric, somehow seems appropriate. The cutting out of designs from printed and figured fabrics for use in quilts was a technique much used in colonial times.

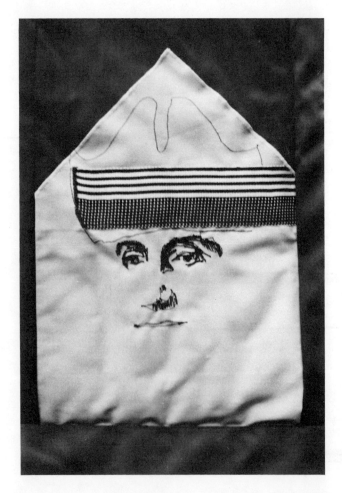

Fig. 3.22 *Happy Birthday, America.*
Detail: George Washington portrait.

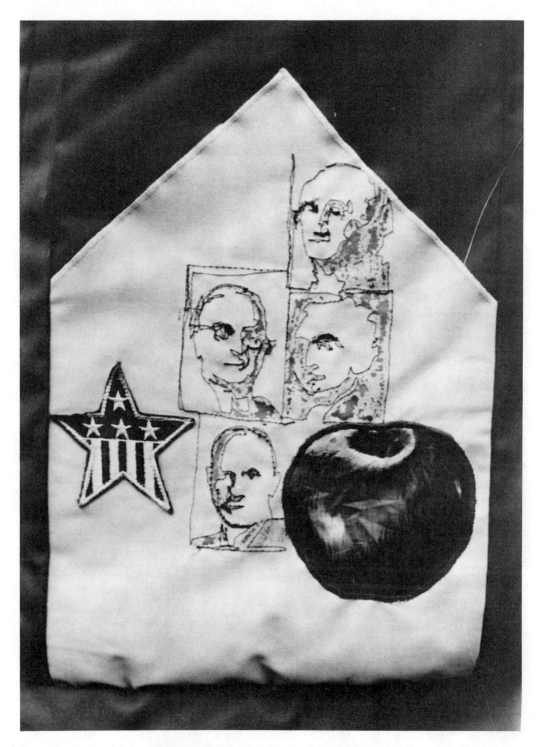

Fig. 3.23 *Happy Birthday, America*. Detail: Presidential portraits.

The dolls in Figures 3.24, 3.25, and 3.26 (detail), based on nineteenth century printed and fabric dolls, illustrate yet another use for machine drawings. The dolls have a very simple shape with appliqued fabric and lace on the dresses and the facial features put on with sewing machine drawings. These children's toys are easy to make, very quick, and suitable for the youngest child. They are also a good use for bits and pieces of nice fabrics and lace. Patterns are included for the dolls with

Fig. 3.24 Two Victorian dolls made in two parts—face and arms, and dress (author).

Fig. 3.25   Victorian dolls. Made with elongated U-shaped
sewn/drawn faces (author).

Fig. 3.26   Detail. Sewn/drawn faces of dolls (author).

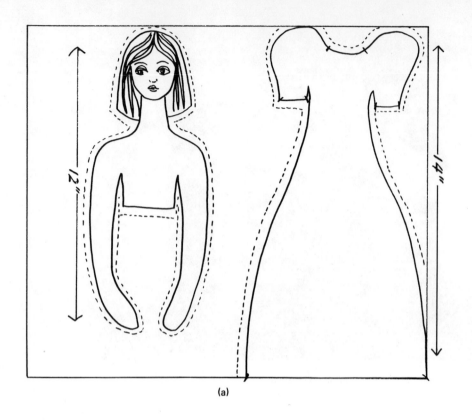

(a)

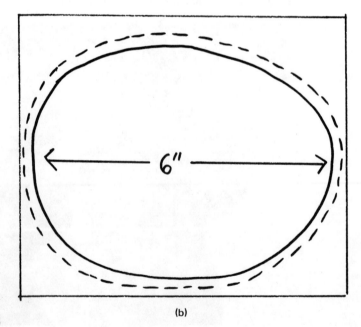

(b)

(c)

Fig. 3.27 (a,b,c) DIRECTIONS FOR VICTORIAN DOLL PATTERN

1. Enlarge design proportionally so that pieces correspond to inch markings on pattern.

2. Select suitable material—anything for dress, closely woven cotton or muslin for head and arms.

3. Cut two of dress piece. (Seam allowances are indicated by dotted line.) Decorate dress pieces with appliqués, old lace, buttons, or ribbons. Place right sides together and sew except at neck, sleeve ends, and bottom.

4. Cut two of doll torso. Transfer face to back of one with pencil (full-size face drawing included). Sew over sketched lines with black thread in needle and bobbin. Bobbin side will be right side. Place right sides together and sew, leaving bottom of torso open.

5. Stuff doll torso with dacron batting or fiberfill.

6. Put doll into dress and stuff dress.

7. Sew doll and dress together at neck and sleeves. Do this by hand, turning edges to make small hem as you go.

8. Cut one round circular bottom piece, and sew by hand onto bottom of dress.

the arms so that you can try some to see how quickly they can be produced (Fig. 3.27). These patterns are not necessarily to **67** be taken as absolutes, but should be changed in any way you see fit. Figure 3.28 shows a doll face before it is cut out. By looking closely you can see that the right side of the face is the bobbin side of the fabric. You can see the textured lines and loops.

The butterfly drawing by the author in Figure 3.29 is an example of a sewn drawing done without a preliminary sketch. It will be one of a series of twenty, each slightly different, that will form the center of a patchwork quilt. Figure 3.30, another of the author's experimental pieces, has a drawing done over a transfer of a magazine image. The image was transferred to fabric, and the drawing was then done on top of it without adhering too closely to the contours of the form. Drawings can be done with the zig-zag stitch on the machine just as easily as with the straight stitch. Figure 3.31 is an example of the zig-zag stitch. (The procedure is exactly the same as that for straight

Fig. 3.28 Detail of doll face (bobbin side) before being cut out (author).

Drawing

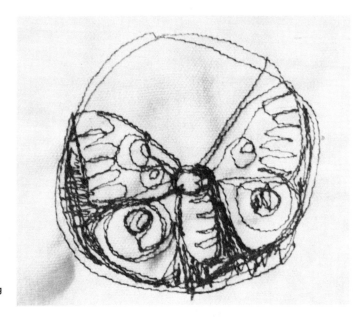

Fig. 3.29 Butterfly. Drawing
on cotton (author).

Fig. 3.30 Drawing over transfer of magazine image (author).

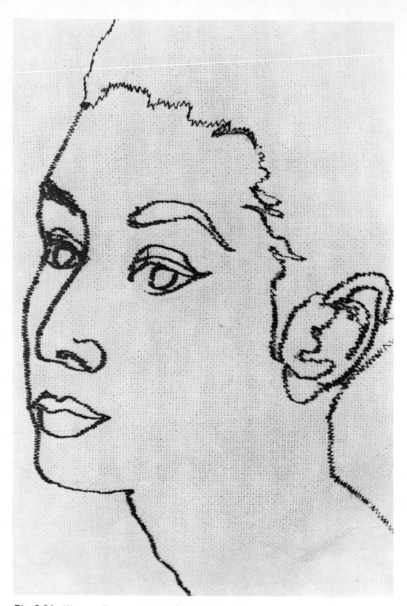

Fig. 3.31   Woman. Zig-zag drawing (author).

stitch drawings.) The only difference is in appearance, because the zig-zag line is considerably thicker.

Experimental drawings are perhaps the most fun to do. Shelly Spiro's piece, Figure 3.32, is an example of a drawing with appliqué. The drawn lines completely cover the appliqués **70** and thereby hold them in place and add textural areas. You can

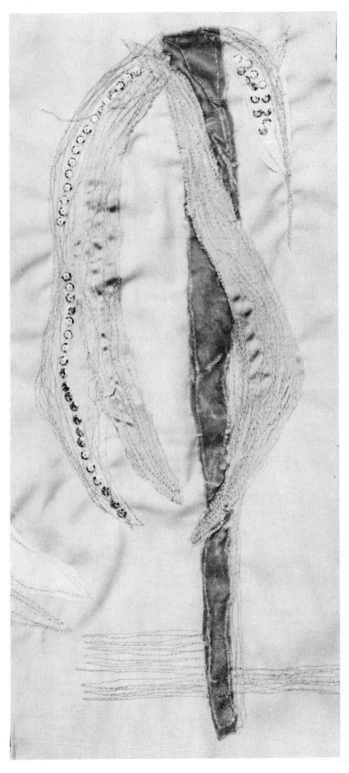

Fig. 3.32 Experimental piece
(Rochelle Spiro).

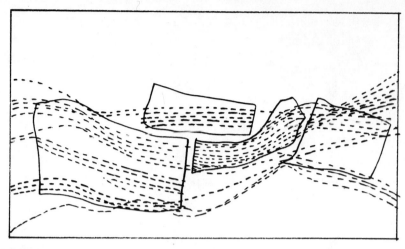

Fig. 3.33

see that the drawn lines are completely at random, much as a scribbled line done with a pen or pencil. When pieces of fabric are layered on the surface of a background, the covering of the top pieces with random lines of straight stitches is a good way

Fig. 3.34 Typewriter. Drawing on satin (Cathy Canfield).

to keep the fabric in place, to build up textural areas, and to create guides for simple drawings (see Fig. 3.33). The two sewn drawings by Cathy Canfield, Figure 3.34, "Typewriter," and Figure 3.35, "Wedding Portrait," were both done on satin fabric. Cathy used light pencil sketches as guidelines, and the drawings that you see are the ones on the bobbin side or underside of the fabric. You can see again the nice thick and thin lines and the uneven line quality that are apparent on the bobbin side. The wedding portrait will be a part of a soft stuffed wedding album that will have a drawing of this type on every page.

The next two drawings, Figures 3.36 and 3.37, illustrate how a sewing machine drawing can be not only freely done and attractive, but also reversible. In Figure 3.36 you can see that the

Fig. 3.35 *Wedding Reception.* Drawing on satin (Cathy Canfield).

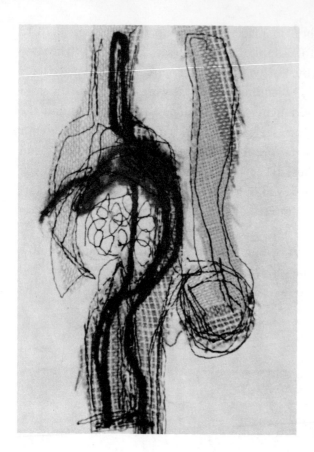

Fig. 3.36 Appliqué with drawing—reversible piece (author).

appliqué pieces were pinned on, and the drawn lines were randomly drawn over the appliqué pieces. The drawn sewn lines sometimes follow the contours of the fabric and sometimes weave in and out between the appliqué pieces and the background. (If you can choose to do a drawing with fabric pieces as guides, the pieces will, of course, have to be facing up.) There is also some wool yarn couched on. Any linear element (yarn, thin rope, twine, plastic tubing, and strands of fabric) can be attached to the surface of the piece with either a straight or a zig-zag stitch. This is, again, the couching technique (see Fig. 3.33). Bits and pieces of other kinds of things can also be attached with the couching technique—bits of torn felt, wads of fabric, bits of fur, and metal wires. Figure 3.37 is the back of the previous plate. You can see that it has the appearance of a very loose drawing, with the thick and thin stitches and the

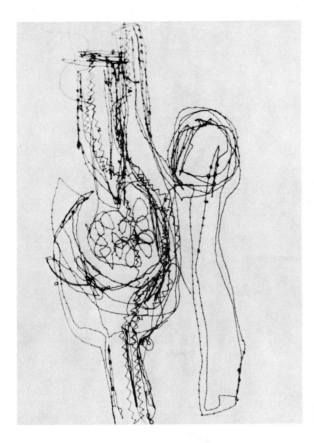

Fig. 3.37 Reverse of appliqué with drawing (author).

bobbin thread loops. It was made to be seen from both sides. This technique of making two-sided pieces could be very usable in window pieces and room dividers. If you wish to do drawings but don't know where to start, perhaps a good way to start would be to add some fabric pieces to a background and use the applied pieces as guides.

Figure 3.38 gives a better idea of the couching technique. This technique can be used with sewn drawings or independently. It shows couching with a straight and a zig-zag stitch. The stitching down of yarns can be done either at random or over previously drawn lines. Figure 3.39 shows a piece in progress. The yarn is laid down, about 2 inches at a time, over a sketched pencil line. The yarn will eventually cover all of the pencil sketch, tacked down with the zig-zag stitch. Figure 3.40 **75** illustrates a vest from Pakistan. It, too, uses the couching

Fig. 3.38 Couching with straight and zig-zag stitches.

Fig. 3.39 Couching piece in progress.

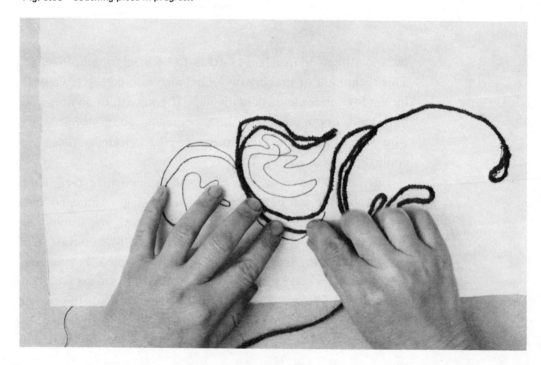

Fig. 3.40 Wedding vest from Pakistan (collection of
Sally Kinsey).

technique, this time with the straight stitch. A flat braid is used
here, and the braid is stitched down and makes a very effective
raised pattern on the surface of the black velvet background
fabric. There are thousands of possibilities for this technique—
to build up patterns, to use it with sewn drawings as an accent,
or to do a complete sewn drawing with this technique are just a
77 few.

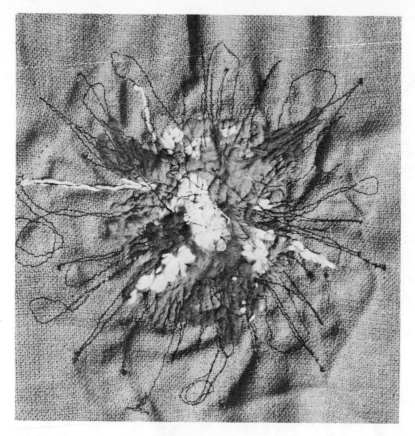

Fig. 3.41 Experimental form. Cotton and wool yarns couched
down to cotton background with drawing stitches
(Sally Kinsey).

The last illustration, Figure 3.41, by Sally Kinsey, shows how
a sewn drawing can be done over groups of yarns that have been
laid on the surface. This is an experimental piece which
illustrates nicely how textural areas can be worked up with
sewn drawings. In this figure, also, you can see how the sewn
lines sometimes are contained within the form and sometimes
overlap the form and wander to the background.

It is hoped, now, that no matter how you draw or think you
draw, you will try the very fascinating technique of sewn
drawings.

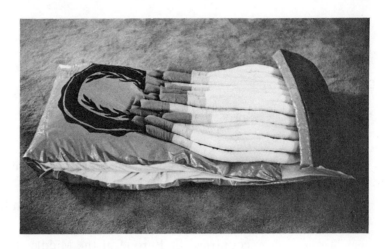

4 Quilting

*It was from Aunt Dinah's Quilting Party
I was seeing Nelly home.*

—Early American folk song

Almost everything that could be done at "Aunt Dinah's quilting party" can be done just as easily and in many cases much more quickly on the standard home sewing machine.

Quilting is one of the oldest of the needlework techniques, and one of the easiest to master. In its most basic form, quilting means the making of a fabric sandwich—a layer of filling or batting between two layers of fabric (see Fig. 4.1).

The origins of quilting have been lost in antiquity, but it is very easy to guess at its evolution. Quilting makes a very warm fabric because the layer of filling or batting traps a layer of air

79

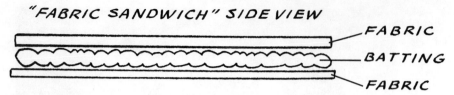

"FABRIC SANDWICH" SIDE VIEW

FABRIC

BATTING

FABRIC

Fig. 4.1 "Fabric sandwich" diagram. Side view.

next to the body. The word quilt comes from the French word *cuilte,* meaning a kind of mattress.

Quilted fabrics have been found in archeological sites from the Middle East to China, and from Peru to the Scandinavian countries. In Europe in the Middle Ages, knights wore quilted doublets under their armor to protect their skin against the chain mail and to protect their upper bodies from superficial blows. In modern China, quilted garments are still the main protection against the cold, as they have been for hundreds of years. In Colonial American times, long before central heating, quilts were the most important bed covering, and they formed one of the main portions of almost every bride's hope chest. They were also given as gifts to politicians and ministers, and as going-away gifts when families or preachers moved from communities. The "quilting bee," the communal get-togethers where the quilting was done, was one of the main social occasions for isolated farm women and city women alike, well into the twenteith century.

There has been a tremendous Renaissance in the art of quilting in the last ten years, partly because it is such an easy and satisfying craft and partly because it gives such a marvelous product—whether it's a standard quilt, a skirt, a jacket, a toy, or any of the other products that are easily adaptable to the quilting technique.

The quilting stitches, the little running stitches that hold the "fabric sandwich" together, done by hand for so many hundreds of years, are now easily done by sewing machine. In fact, not only do they hold the three layers together, but they add a decorative element, and in many cases accentuate the patchwork or appliqué top by outlining it so that it stands out in relief or by adding a supplementary pattern to the negative areas.

Many things have been used historically to fill quilts (to be the middle of the "fabric sandwich"). One of the most common until the twentieth century was bats of combed wool fibers (the fibers after they were corded). From those fibers we get the word "batting," which is used interchangeably today with the words "filling" or "padding." Sometimes the wool bats were cleaned, and sometimes they retained the very pungent sheep smell of the raw wool! At other times, the quilts were filled with corn husks, cotton, old quilts, old clothes or rags, newspapers, blankets, or feathers and down.

As mentioned previously, quilting can be used in the production of more than the standard bed-covering quilt. Jackets, pants, handbags, rugs, hats, skirts, hangings, upholstery fabrics, and jewelry are a few of the things that can be made using the quilting technique.

Quiltmakers practiced recycling long before it became a popular practice. And the use of old cloths, old curtains, remnants of fabrics, and bits and pieces of thrift shop junk greatly enhances quilted pieces and adds to the fun of the execution—not to mention the price! In some circles I'm known as the crazy girl who likes old flowered drapes and doilies!

As mentioned previously, almost everything that could be done by hand in times past can now be done by sewing machine. Results similar to those of the projects pictured in this section can be duplicated by studying the illustrations carefully.

I have divided the quilting techniques into three distinct types. These categories are not absolute, but simply one quilter's way of categorizing the quilter's craft.

The three main methods are:

1. *Standard or English quilting.* This is the most common quilting method, the one with the "fabric sandwich"—a top and a bottom layer of fabric and a center layer of batting, held together with stitches. Most quilts that you would be familiar with were probably done using this method.

2. *Padded quilting or Trapunto.* This is the method of quilting used when only particular areas in a piece are stuffed or quilted. In a

trapunto or padded piece you will see only part of the design in relief. This is also the method, used in conjunction with the standard method, that you would use if you wished to overstuff particular areas in a quilt.

3. *Corded or Italian quilting.* This is the quilting method used when raised linear patterns are required on the surface of a piece. Parallel lines are sewn in a design, and cords or multiple yarns are threaded through the parallel lines, making linear patterns in relief.

Before we go on, a word should be inserted here about materials. Fabrics that are most suitable for quilting, no matter what the end product will be, are closely woven cottons, cotton blends, satins, taffetas, velvets, velveteens, and corduroys. Stretch fabrics and double knits are not as easily used for quilting because of their tendency to stretch. They are also generally harder to control. Again, these suggestions are not absolute; they are just bits of wisdom picked up from bad experiences.

There are three commodities, besides my sewing machine, that I really couldn't do without in my work—a dishwasher (to save time and free me of a horrid task), masking tape, and dacron batting and fiberfill. I have found the dacron batting to be superior to cotton batting. It is light-weight, stays together as a bat, is washable, non-allergenic, and comes rolled in the standard bed and comforter sizes. The fiberfill comes packaged by the pound and is used to stuff objects, such as toys, that are not flat.

The best kinds of thread to use are the standard cotton threads, or the quilting threads that are for sale in some areas.

STANDARD QUILTING METHOD

Three layers are used in the standard quilting method—top, lining, and batting (see Fig. 4.2). These directions are for a square or rectangular quilt.

Step 1. Have your quilt top finished. It can be patchwork, appliqué, or combinations of those or any other techniques.

Step 2. Iron both the quilt top and the lining (which should be the same size as the top).

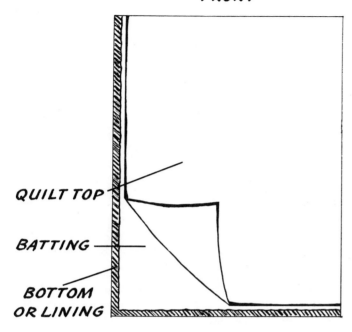

STANDARD OR ENGLISH QUILTING

FRONT

QUILT TOP

BATTING

BOTTOM
OR LINING

SIDE VIEW

TOP

BATTING

BOTTOM

Fig. 4.2 Standard or English quilting.

Step 3. On a large clean surface, lay your lining out, face down. Unroll the batting, and lay it over the lining. When you have completed that step, lay the quilt top over the batting, face up.

Step 4. Carefully baste the three layers together. See Figure 4.3 for the direction of basting stitches. A note should be inserted here: any sewing machine will sew two layers of fabric and one layer of batting. Most will not sew through four or five layers of batting. If you want some especially puffy area, it would be best to supplement this technique with the trapunto technique, covered later in this chapter.

Step 5. If your quilting stitches are going to follow the outline of an appliqué or patchwork design, you will need no marking. However, if your quilting lines are going to form a pattern in either the negative or positive areas of your design, you will need to mark your quilting lines

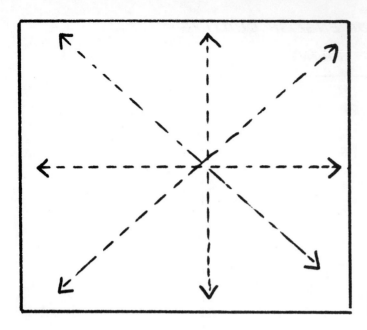

Fig. 4.3   Step 4 diagram.
Directions of basting stitches.

on the top of the quilt with either chalk or dressmaker's carbon. (These substances will wear off in time or come out in the wash.) If your lines are parallel or if they form geometric patterns, they can be put on with a yardstick as a guide. If your quilting design calls for curving or asymmetrical lines, you can draw them on randomly, or you can cut a template from a plastic bleach bottle or a styrofoam meat holder and draw around your template many times to get your repeat pattern. See Figure 4.4 for possible quilting patterns. Some machines come equipped with extra equipment, and one of the pieces often included is a quilting foot, which gives the sewer guides for sewing parallel lines. This is a good foot to use in place of the standard presser foot if your quilting design calls for straight lines.

Step 6. Set the thread tension to the tension for a heavy fabric. (You can check your instruction booklet for this.) Set your stitch length for 8 to 10 stitches per inch. Check your needle to make certain that it's very sharp. The color of thread you use can match or contrast with the quilt top.

Step 7a. Quilting in straight lines: If your quilting pattern is based on straight lines (grids, diamond shapes, squares, rectangles, or any other geometric shape with straight sides), you will want to sew over your quilting lines just as you would for any straight seam—with the feed dog up in its regular position and with the regular pressure on the presser foot.

Step 7b. Quilting in curving or asymmetrical lines: If you are quilting in curving lines, or perhaps following the lines of your design on your quilt top, you will want to put the feed dog down and release

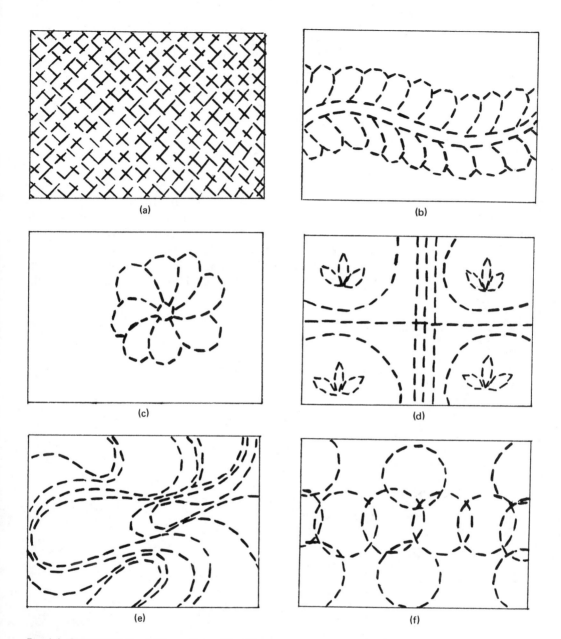

Fig. 4.4 Possibilities for quilting patterns (Step 5).
(a) Done with yardstick; (b,c,d,f) done with templates;
(e) done randomly.

half the pressure on the presser foot. (This is, again, the setting for "darning" on most machines. The feed dog has to go down because it feeds the fabric through in a straight line. Half the pressure is left on **85** the presser foot because it holds the fabric down a little better.) You will, of course, lower the presser foot. Setting your machine like this will allow you to move your fabric in any direction you wish.

Step 8. If your piece is large in area, some agility is required to get it both under the presser foot and under the arm of the machine. As suggested previously, have a large area on which to work. (This may mean setting chairs or tables next to your machine so that your quilt does not fall on the floor.) The best technique to follow is to quilt the right side of the quilt from the edge to the center, then take the quilt out, turn it around, and quilt the left side from edge to center, making sure you overlap the quilting stitches slightly where they meet in the middle (see Fig. 4.5). If the fabric already quilted becomes too cumbersome under the arm of the machine, roll it into a tight roll, pin it with large safety pins, and it should slide easily under the machine arm (see Fig. 4.6). When you are doing your sewn quilting, do not try to make the machine stitch quickly, or you will lose control. A slower than normal speed is best. You should also only concentrate on the

Fig. 4.5 Direction of quilt stitches from both sides to center of quilt (Step 8).

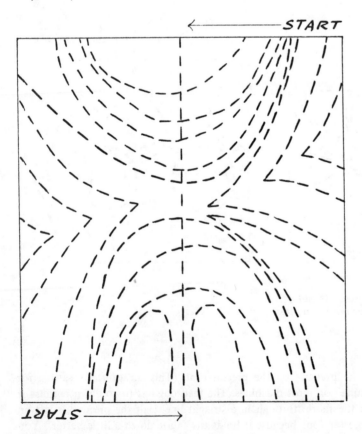

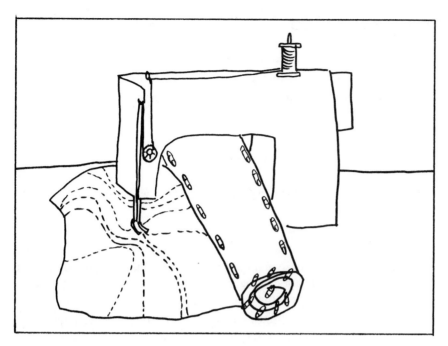

Fig. 4.6 Step 8 diagram. Quilt rolled up and secured with safety
pins and the roll put under the machine arm.

small area you are sewing on at any one time, working with both hands
to guide the fabric and keep it straight and flat.

Step 9. When you have completed the quilting, it doesn't hurt to
lightly press the entire piece again, although it isn't absolutely
necessary.

Step 10. When all of your quilting is completed, you are ready to
finish the edges. This can be done in a number of ways:

a. Finish the edges with blanket binding, according to the
directions on the package.

b. Finish the edges by turning them in, pinning them, and sewing
them by hand or by machine.

c. Finish the edges by cutting bias strips about 2 1/2″ to 3″ wide
in the same or contrasting fabric, and sew them together to make a
strip long enough to go around the quilt. Fold this bias strip in half
lengthwise, and sew the raw edges to the lining side about 1/4″ from
the edge. Then turn the quilt right side up, fold the doubled strip
over the edge, and stitch it down.

Note: for any standard flat quilt, the batting should be sewn down
every 8 to 10 inches in some manner to prevent it from shifting or
bunching.

PADDED QUILTING OR TRAPUNTO

Two layers of fabric and fiberfill are used in padded quilting. Trapunto is used when you want only certain areas stuffed, or when you want some parts of your design overstuffed.

Step 1. Have your quilt top finished. It can be done in any technique, or left plain.

Step 2. Iron both the top and the lining (which should be the same size).

Step 3. Make the design on your quilt top with dressmaker's carbon, pencil, or chalk.

Step 4. Baste the two layers together—bottom layer face down, top layer face up.

Step 5. Sew over your quilting lines, using the same procedures as in Step 5 for standard quilting. Step 6, Steps 7a or 7b, and Step 8 apply equally to this trapunto method.

Step 6. When all sewn quilting lines are completed, turn quilt over so that the lining is on top, and make small cuts with your scissors in the center of areas that you want stuffed. Stuff fiberfill into these areas with a pencil or crochet hook, making sure that the batting gets into all the little corners (see Fig. 4.7). A close-up is shown in Figure 4.8. When all the areas are stuffed to your satisfaction, sew them up again with a whip stitch.

This technique can be used in connection with standard quilting if you have one particular area that you want to overstuff. You simply slit the particular area from the back, add stuffing to the batting already there (following the directions in Step 6), and close the slit with the whip stitch.

This technique can be used for whole quilts or for small areas like the center of jackets or pillow tops.

CORDED QUILTING OR ITALIAN QUILTING

Corded quilting is used when you want raised linear patterns on the surface of your piece, whether it's a quilt, a pillow, a hanging, or a garment.

Materials used here are two layers of fabric and cotton piping, cotton cord, or multiple strands of yarn, and a large **88** blunt needle.

Fig. 4.7   Back of work (Step 6).
Areas that are to be stuffed have
small cuts in them. The batting is
then stuffed in with a pencil or
crochet hook.

Fig. 4.8   Padded quilting or trapunto back of work—close-up.
(a) Stuffing a particular area. (b) The slit sewn up with a whip
stitch.

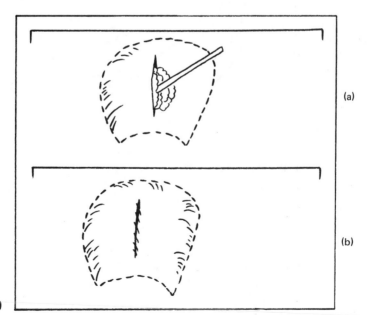

(a)

(b)

Step 1. Have your quilt top finished. It can be done in any technique, or left plain.

Step 2. Iron both the top and the lining.

Step 3. Mark the design on your quilt top with dressmaker's carbon, pencil, or chalk. Your design should be done in parallel lines, each line 1/8″, 1/4″, or 3/8″ apart from the other, depending on the type of cord to be threaded through the parallel lines. These parallel lines can be straight or curved, and can form any type of design (see Fig. 4.9).

Step 4. Baste the top and lining together—bottom layer face down, top layer face up.

Step 5. Sew over your quilting lines, using the same procedure as in Step 5 for standard quilting. Step 6, Steps 7a or 7b, and Step 8 apply equally to this corded quilting.

Step 6. You are now ready to thread cords or piping or multiple yarns through the parallel lines.

Step 7. Thread your cords onto a large blunt needle.

Step 8. Make or find an opening and put your needle through. The needle will go easily through straight or gently curving lines (see Fig. 4.10). If you have sharp curves or square corners, you will need to cut a tiny hole at the sharp corners and bring your needle out at these

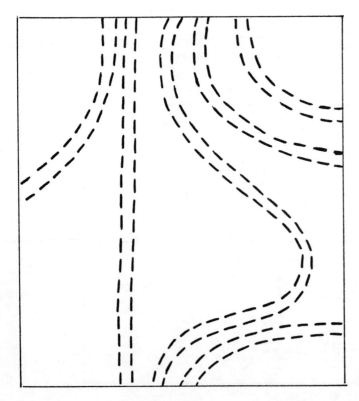

Fig. 4.9 Diagram of back of work illustrating parallel lines ready to be threaded with cord.

Quilting

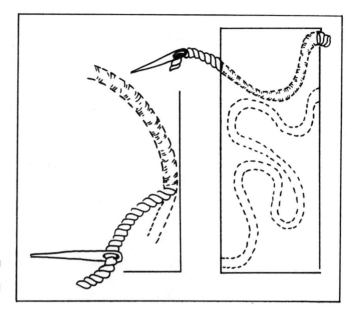

Fig. 4.10 Back of work. Corded quilting with sharp angles. Thread has to come out and go in again because needle will not go around sharp turns.

corners, putting them back in about 1/16″ from where the needle came out, leaving a little loop of yarn so that the piece will not pucker (see Fig. 4.11).

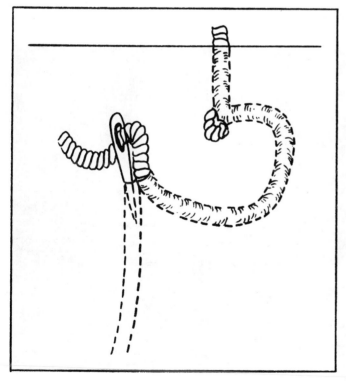

Fig. 4.11 Diagram of corded or Italian quilting (back of work)—close-up.

Step 9. When all the parallel lines have been threaded, stitch the ends of the cords to the back of the piece by hand.

Quilting can be used for three-dimensional sculptural pieces as well as the standard quilts and garments. Jeannie Ilgen's piece, "Syracuse University Matchbook Bed," is not only a quilted sculpture, but also a utilitarian object. When the top of the matchbook is opened, it becomes a very comfortable mattress on which to sit or lie. The fabrics used are vinyl for the outside and closely woven cotton for the inside and the matches. It is a marvelously humorous comment on furniture. The piece has a wonderful vitality. Where else could you rest your head on twenty matches? The artist made this piece because she was going away from Syracuse University to graduate school and needed pieces of light, portable furniture. Figure 4.12 shows the piece with the matches out, and Figure 4.13 shows the piece with the matches inside the cover. The next two illustrations (Figs. 4.14 and 4.15) are asymmetrical drawings that serve to hold the two layers of fabric and one

Fig. 4.12 Syracuse University Matchbook Bed, view 1 (Jeannie Ilgen).

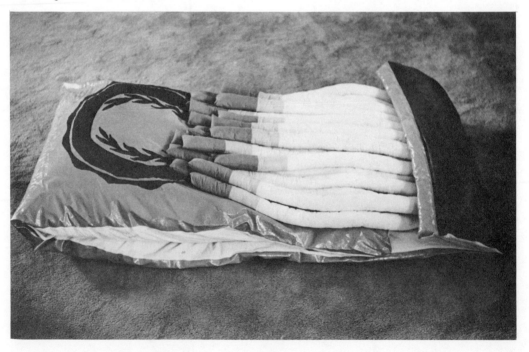

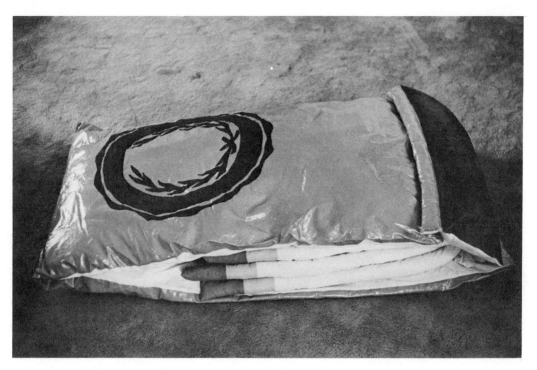

Fig. 4.13 Syracuse University Matchbook Bed, view 2.

Fig. 4.14 Small quilted experiment. Cotton
with dacron batting; an asymmetrical quilting
pattern, Step 7b for standard quilting
(author).

Fig. 4.15 Small quilted experiment. Cotton with dacron batting; an asymmetrical free-quilted design, Step 7b for standard quilting (author).

layer of batting together; they were experiments done by the author to illustrate the fact that quilted pieces need not have any appliqué or decoration on their surface. The quilting lines themselves can be the whole design. (These two pieces were done according to the directions for Step 7b in the section on standard quilting.)

Jeannie Ilgen's quilt "Calypso" (Fig. 4.16) is an example of the surface embellishment of a quilted piece both by the patchwork areas (with all the fabrics sewn by machine in the patchwork technique, edge to edge) and by the quilting lines. All the details on the face and hands are arrived at by the sewing machine quilting lines. Again, the directions for this technique are contained in the section on standard quilting, especially Step 7b. The piece has a very successful dark and

light pattern which makes the main shapes especially dramatic.

95   Fig. 4.16 *Calypso Quilt* (Jeannie Ilgen).

Fig. 4.17 *Candy Store*. Quilted hanging (Barbara Gentry).

The piece has one layer of dacron batting and a lining of closely woven cotton. All of the shapes stand out in relief because the artist not only quilted inside all the shapes (the details on the head and hands) but also quilted around all the individual shapes to insure their dimensional quality.

Barbara Gentry's quilted hanging "Candy Store" (Fig. 4.17) utilizes all three of the main quilting techniques quite successfully—standard, trapunto, and corded quilting. It is a white-on-white piece done entirely of muslin and stuffed with dacron batting. Many of the quilted shapes were done separately and sewn on—a good idea if you have some shapes that cannot be executed easily on a flat surface. The overstuffed (trapunto) straight lines serve to accentuate the squares they define and to call further attention to the nicely patterned shapes they contain. The two details (Figs. 4.18 and 4.19) of this piece allow you more easily to distinguish the quilting lines.

The quilted neckpiece by the author, Figure 4.20, shows that quilting can be used for body jewelry and small pieces as well as the larger pieces. It is constructed of closely woven cotton, and the quilting lines are freely stitched on the top. It has one layer of batting and is set with a synthetic ruby, although a nice button would have done just as well. The beaded fringe on the bottom of the piece was trim from a 1920s dress. Small items such as this are very nice to practice on because they are quick and easy to make and many times will give you ideas for larger pieces.

Sally Kinsey's quilted floor form, Figure 4.21, is made from burlap sewn into an elongated triangle and has bits of yarn coming out from an opening in the top. Machine-stitched lines provide pattern on the top and the bottom of the piece. This quilted sculptural piece spent a long time under an old rocking chair of mine, and it had a vaguely sinister look about it whenever anyone came into the room. Figure 4.22, a detail of a quilt by Marsha Zambakian, shows how quilting lines that follow the lines of the appliqué shapes make the individual shapes stand out in relief. Extra quilting was done in the larger area to make sure that all the batting was tacked down at least every 6 to 8 inches. The piece is made from closely woven

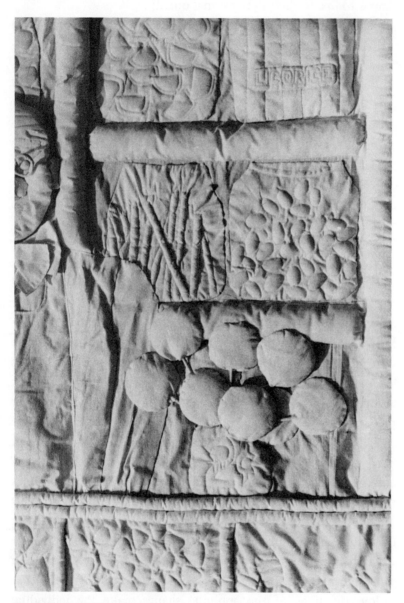

Fig. 4.18 *Candy Store.* Detail 1.

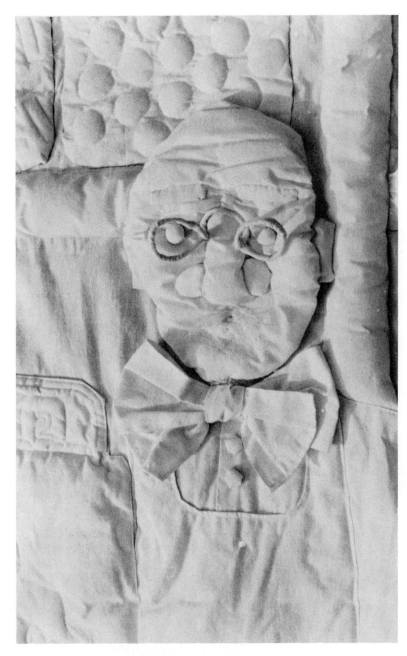

Fig. 4.19 *Candy Store*. Detail 2.

Fig. 4.20 Neckpiece—quilted (author).

Fig. 4.21 Quilted floor form (Sally Kinsey)

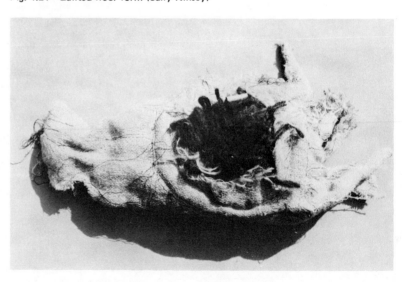

Fig. 4.22 Quilt—detail (Marsha Zambakian Watson).

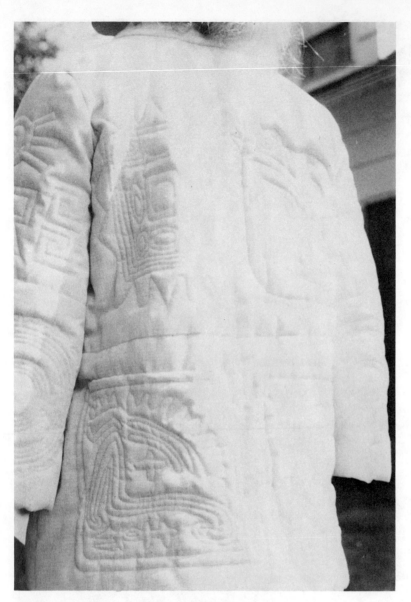

Fig. 4.23 Quilted jacket—detail (Laurene Piston).

cottons, and it is put together with one layer of batting which makes it completely washable. The design here is quite simple but very effective.

Laurene Piston used a commercial jacket pattern to get the basic shapes for her jacket, pictured in Figures 4.23 and 4.24. A closely woven cotton was chosen for the fabric, and the quilting was done with a very thin muslin as the back layer. The pieces were cut out individually and quilted, with the quilt lines transferred to the fabric with dressmaker's carbon. The quilting was done with a matching thread, so that there is no change of color in the piece, just a change in depth from the high and low relief of the quilted shapes. The whole piece was lined upon completion with a matching crepe and a zipper was put up the front. The jacket is very light and extremely warm, and is also washable. The quilted shapes are based on pre-Columbian textile and ceramic design motifs.

Fig. 4.24 Quilted jacket—front (Laurene Piston).

I hope that the photographs and the information in the preceding chapters have helped you look at your sewing machine in a new light—as a wonderfully versatile and extremely enjoyable tool. The main thing to remember is that sewing is first and foremost *fun* and that whatever you do is right. I can only hope that this book sets you on a trail similar to mine, leading to a room full of old fabrics and remnants, thread of every color, old buttons, and ribbons and lace, and hundreds of ideas for my next projects. Never mind the bedroom moss that occurs with great regularity under every piece of furniture and the dreariness of our dinners, usually made up of one of the two dishes in my cooking repertoire—corned beef sandwiches and spaghetti! Never mind the unanswered letters and the windows with the greasy little fingerprints—there are *sewings* to be done!

Glossary

Appliqué. From the French *Appliquer*, meaning "to put on." In fabric terms, it means a decorated piece whose design is arrived at by fabrics shapes attached to a background by means of stitches.

Backing. The lining or bottom layer of an appliqué, a quilt, or any fabric piece having a top and bottom, or front and back.

Batting. The middle layer of a quilt or quilted piece. Usually a specially manufactured 1/2″ to 1″ layer of nonwoven cotton or dacron polyester fibers. Can also be old blankets or rags.

Binding. A method of finishing off edges of appliqués or quilts by attaching commercial blanket binding or bias strips along all sides to cover raw edges.

Closely woven cloth. Fabric which has sufficient threads per inch in both warp and weft to make it strong and able to take much wear. Examples would be denim, poplin, kettle cloth, and Indian head.

Corded quilting (Italian quilting). A technique in which two pieces of fabric are put together, and parallel lines are sewn in a design on the surface, connecting the two pieces of fabric. Heavy cords or yarns are then threaded through the parallel lines, creating raised linear patterns.

Couch, to. In machine stitchery, a technique by which heavy cords or yarns are attached to the surface of a piece by means of the wide-apart zig-zag stitch.

Coverlet. A bed cover, often quilted, usually one-half to three-quarters the size of the bed.

Ease in, to. To gently push or pull fabric to its place in an appliqué or quilted piece.

Filler. See batting.

Hem. To turn the raw edges of a fabric piece under, or to the inside.

Miter. To join two pieces of fabric together at the corners with a 45-degree angle where they come together.

Muslin. A common plain woven cotton fabric, usually with an egg-shell color, which comes in many weights from sheer to heavy.

Padding. See batting.

Patchwork. A technique in which fabric pieces of various sizes and shapes are sewn together edge to edge to form either random or specific patterns.

Piece, to. To put together a fabric unit using the patchwork technique.

Quilt. A "fabric sandwich" usually consisting of a top design layer, a middle layer of batting, and a bottom layer of lining. Can be used as bed covers, garments, or decorative pieces.

Quilt, to. To sew the three layers of the "fabric sandwich" together with either hand or machine stitches.

Stuffing. See batting.

Trapunto. A method of quilting in which a particular area in a quilt is overstuffed by slitting the area from the back, adding extra stuffing, and sewing the slit up again.

Wadding. See batting.

Bibliography

Belfer, Nancy. *Designing in Stitching and Appliqué*. Worcester, Mass.: David Publications, Inc., 1972.

Dean, Beryl. *Creative Appliqué*. New York: Watson-Guptill Publications, 1970.

Gonsalves, Alyson Smith (Ed.). *Quilting and Patchwork*. Menlo Park, Calif.: Lane Books, 1973.

Gray, Jennifer. *Machine Embroidery, Technique and Design*. New York: Van Nostrand Reinhold Co., 1973.

Guild, Vera P. *New Complete Book of Needlecraft*. New York: Good Housekeeping Books, 1959.

Hall, Carolyn Vosburg. *Stitched and Stuffed Art*. Garden City, New York: Doubleday & Co., 1974.

109

Bibliography

Kretsinger, Rose G., and Hall, Carrie A. *The Romance of the Patchwork Quilt.* New York: Bonanza Books, 1935.

Laliberte, Norman, and McIlhany, Sterling. *Banners and Hangings.* New York: Van Nostrand Reinhold Co., 1966.

Laury, Jean Ray. *Appliqué Stitchery.* New York: Reinhold Publishing Corp., 1966.

Laury, Jean Ray. *Doll Making: A Creative Approach.* New York: Van Nostrand Reinhold, N.D.

Laury, Jean Ray. *Quilt and Coverlets. A Contemporary Approach.* New York: Van Nostrand Reinhold, 1970.

Laury, Jean Ray, and Aiken, Joyce. *Creative Body Coverings.* New York: Van Nostrand Reinhold, 1973.

Leman, Bonnie. *Quick and Easy Quilting.* Great Neck, New York: Hearthside Press, Inc., 1972.

Lewis, Alfred Allan. *The Mountain Artisans Quilting Book.* New York: Macmillan Publishing Co., 1973.

McCall's Needlework and Crafts. *McCall's How to Quilt It.* New York: McCall Pattern Co., N.D.

McKim, Ruby. *101 Patchwork Patterns.* New York: Dover Publications, Inc., 1962.

Marein, Shirley. *Stitchery, Needlepoint, Appliqué, and Patchwork, A Complete Guide.* New York: The Viking Press, 1974.

Meilach, Dona Z. *Soft Sculpture and Other Soft Art Forms.* New York: Crown Publications, Inc., 1974.

Meilach, Dona Z., and Snow, Lee Erlin. *Creative Stitchery.* Chicago: Reilly and Lee, 1970.

Murray, Aileen. *Design in Fabric and Thread.* New York: Watson-Guptill Publications, 1969.

110

Bibliography

Rainey, Sarita R. *Wall Hangings: Designing with Fabric and Thread.* Worcester, Mass.: David Publications, Inc., 1971.

Shears, Evangeline, and Fielding, Diantha. *Appliqué.* New York: Watson-Guptill Publications, 1972.

Wilcox, Donald J. *New Design in Stitchery.* New York: Van Nostrand Reinhold, 1970.

Wooster, Ann Sargent. *Quiltmaking: A Modern Approach to a Traditional Craft.* New York: Drake Publishers, Inc., 1972.

Index